Money Laundering and Terrorist Financing Activities

Money Laundering and Terrorist Financing Activities

A Primer on Avoidance Management for Money Managers

Milan Frankl

Ayse Ebru Kurcer

BEP BUSINESS EXPERT PRESS

Money Laundering and Terrorist Financing Activities: A Primer on Avoidance Management for Money Managers
Copyright © Business Expert Press, LLC, 2017.

First published in 2017 by
Business Expert Press, LLC
222 East 46th Street, New York, NY 10017
www.businessexpertpress.com

ISBN-13: 978-1-63157-593-8 (print)
ISBN-13: 978-1-63157-594-5 (e-book)

Business Expert Press Finance and Financial Management Collection

Collection ISSN: 2331-0049 (print)
Collection ISSN: 2331-0057 (electronic)

Cover and interior design by S4Carlisle Publishing Services Private Ltd., Chennai, India

First edition: 2017

10 9 8 7 6 5 4 3 2 1

Printed in the United States of America

Dedication

To Ebru for her dedication, tenacity, and enthusiasm for participating in writing this book;
to Professor Frankl who has given me his guidance, help and motivation that cleared my path in writing this book and to all the honest and brave people around the world.

Abstract

The purpose of this book is to introduce the reader to mechanisms useful for detection and avoidance of money-laundering activities (MLAs) and terrorist financing and suggest improvements to existing MLAs where appropriate.

Money laundering may occur in every country. The significant factor is to diagnose the illegal MLA and apply regulations to mitigate them. To meet this objective, managers of financial institutions need to train their employees about anti-money laundering (AML) processes and how to diagnose and prevent money laundering.

AML activities can also affect the financial systems of a country. "Money laundering destabilizes the foundation of a nation's financial system by reducing tax revenues and impeding fair competition by ultimately disrupting economic development" (World Compliance, 2008). MLAs can create a big gap between income classes. Money laundering can also decrease banks' or financial institutions' credibility.

"In practice, criminals are trying to disguise the origins of money obtained through illegal activities so that it looks like it was obtained from legal sources" (Layton, 2005).

This book may be of special interest to financial managers in the private and public sector. It also may be a useful guide for those involved in international financial transactions.

Keywords

logistic regression, model building, model diagnostics, multiple regression, regression model, simple linear regression, statistical inference, time series regression

Contents

Acknowledgments

I sincerely thank my graduate student Ebru Kurcer, MBA, for her unwavering effort and dedication to the MBA program and her related research. Ebru faced the research challenges a topic of this nature required and created opportunities to achieve an exceptional experience. Ebru's persistent patience, wit, undisputed sense of humor, motivation, and a guiding light, showed the way on this journey of research and writing of her thesis. A daunting task but doable. She achieved a new level of commitment, a *can do* attitude that transcended work and career.

I kindly thank my MBA Professor, Milan Frankl, who had given me this wonderful opportunity to transform my thesis project into a book that would enlighten many people in the field of finance. Professor Frankl's positive attitude and experiences in the field helped me to overcome any kind of obstacles along the way.

I also would like to thank all the people who have given me their time and knowledge on this particular subject that helped broaden my vision.

CHAPTER 1

Background

Evolution of the Money Laundering Process

In many countries the "unregistered economic values" have been an important issue for the evolution of money-laundering activities. Although clear definition of 'unregistered economy' exists, according to Erdilek, unregistered economy could be associated with:

- Excessive tax burdens,
- Corporate and personal taxes,
- Social security contributions,
- Inflexible labor markets (Erdilek, 2007).

Erdilek adds that 'the reluctance of some people to pay their share of taxes' could be another reason for unregistered economy. He mentions that the reason for the unwillingness of paying the full share of taxes could be that people believe governments are wasting tax revenues.

Economic activities could be defined using the Gross Domestic Product (GDP) index. GDP involves legal and illegal economic activities. For example, according to the Turkish Confederation of Employers' Associations' survey in 2003, 'Turkey's unregistered economy increased from 36 % of the registered economy in 1985 to 66 % in 2003' (Erdilek, 2007). The Turkish Central Bank study in 2004 revealed that the unregistered Turkish economy, (including 52 % of total employment and 37 % of private sector employment), was between 16 to 50 % of total economic activity. In 2005, The Trade Union Turkish-Is reports that 'more than half of the Turkish labor force was engaged in the unregistered economy' (Erdilek, 2007).

Unregistered economies have negative effects on the country's economy. The unwanted effects of the unregistered economy could be listed as follows:

- Official statistics are no longer reliable.
- Financial policies are difficult to develop and implement.
- Companies within the registered economy invest out of the country because of unfair competition.
- Governments need to increase the tax load that results from unregistered taxes.
- The value for the legal foundations of the society decreases.

Besides the negative effects, unregistered taxes have some positive effects on the society and economy: they maintain an additional employment and income opportunity. However, the negative effects of unregistered economy are much greater than the positive ones to people and the country's financial system.

Countries' financial systems may include different methods of illegal fund movement transactions. These fund movements can be considered as a form of unrecorded economy and could include:

- Funds accumulated for tax evasion,
- Funds generated from illegal activities, and
- Funds to be used for terrorist financing.

Even though these three types of fundsare different, at times they partly cover each other's area according to the type of criminal financial activity.

The source of the funds for criminal activities is called 'Black Money'.

The cycle process of black money can be shown as:

Crime ➡ Black Money ➡ Money-Laundering[1]

Criminals launder money to hide the original source of funds that are generated by a criminal activity. The purpose of the activity is to legalize illegal income with an official cover through a variety of methods.

---

[1] **Money laundering** is the process of transforming the proceeds of crime into ostensibly legitimate **money** or other assets.

Hiding money laundering activities can be achieved through:

- Converting dirty money into acceptable form of funds,
- "Washing" the proceeds gained from the drug trade, and
- Formalizing the incomes generated from illegal activities.

Illegal sources of money can be listed as follows:

- Bribing,
- Drug Smuggling,
- Illegal weapon or arms trading,
- Human trading,
- Refugee smuggling, and
- Other unofficial trading activities.

Money laundering gives criminals significant financial power.

In the 1970s, the United States of America implemented the Bank Secrecy Act (BSA)[2] to prevent money laundering-type activities. According to Internal Revenue Service (IRS)'s report in 2011, 'The BSA requires businesses to keep records and file reports that are determined to have a high degree of usefulness in criminal, tax, and regulatory matters'. This act helped also other governments limit terrorist financing activities and control financial transactions.

Financial institutions have a variety of policies and regulations to fight illegal money transactions. These policies help prevent criminals from using individual banks for money laundering transactions. These policies are often referred to as anti-money laundering applications.

Anti-money laundering applications could affect financial institutions' legal positions, and involve compliance costs as well as affect negatively their financial position.

---

[2]The **Bank Secrecy Act** (BSA), also known as the Currency and Foreign Transactions Reporting **Act**, is legislation passed by the United States Congress in 1970 that requires U.S. financial institutions to collaborate with the U.S. government in cases of suspected money laundering and fraud.

Legal Position

Employees in financial institutions are required to follow their organization's rules. Besides following organization's rules, employees are also required to

- Maintain proper record-keeping of financial transactions,
- Maintain internal reporting, and
- Train other employees about legal obligations and report suspicious transactions to management.

Compliance Cost

The compliance costs of financial institutions or services increase when adopting anti-money laundering applications in an organization. These costs consist of administration, training, and storage costs.

Compliance departments within financial institutions are established to monitor the activities of a financial institution and identify possible suspicious transactions within the organization. Financial organizations establish these compliance departments and develop policies required to meet the legal standards and manage clients' assets.

For that reason, banks implement a continuing compliance program to meet their obligations and responsibilities.

Compliance policies regulations and procedures support the fulfillment of anti-money laundering and anti-terrorist financing measures. Those measures are also supported with strict local laws and regulations. In this respect, the functions of Compliance Officers are vital for financial institutions.

According to the 'Bank Regulatory Compliance Officer Job Description' on the website www.advisoryhq.com, the duties of a bank's Compliance Officer are as follows:

- Ensuring that the bank unit operates in compliance with all applicable regulations as well as the internal policies and procedures,
- Implementing bank's Compliance Policies within the unit,
- Providing counsel on regulatory issues and potential effect of regulatory changes,
- Developing, implementing, and revising compliance policies,

- Cooperating daily with local regulatory authorities,
- Ensuring senior management and staff are educated and trained with the bank's compliance policies and procedures,
- Monitoring the bank's compliance unit's activities to detect and prevent possible faults of the agreement,
- Conducting regular internal investigations and providing recommendations to correct some actions,
- Dealing with complaints and maintain objection files and records,
- Managing clients' orders and permissions with written guidelines and restrictions,
- Interacting with members from internal audit, risk management, and financial reporting, and
- Reporting hierarchically to the Management Board and functionally to the Council of Directors.

Financing terrorism and money laundering are related to each other. Money launderers are not always providing funds to terrorist organizations. However, terrorism financing activities need money laundering to legalize their funds and sources.

Money Laundering Stages

Money laundering may look like a simple process that criminals use for hiding the source of the proceeds of their illegal financial criminal activities. However, money laundering has a deep social significance with direct links to corruption in financial organizations.

United Nations Office on Drugs and Crime (UNODC) (See Figure 1.1), states the money laundering process has three stages: Placement, Layering, and Integration.

In the **Placement** stage, the launderer tries to transform the cash into other assets such as postal orders or checks to remove the link between the cash and its source. In the second stage, **Layering**, the goal is to conceal the audit trial, source, and ownership of funds. To achieve that purpose, the launderer disguises the source of the funds by creating complex layers and forming different financial transactions. During the third stage, **Integration**, the launderer assimilates the money with other assets of the financial system.

Under the above scheme, banking systems are at the center of the money laundering processes. Therefore, rules and regulations applied in banking systems are the key factors for fighting money laundering activities.

Money laundering activities, which also can be used as terrorist-financing activities, affect the world's economy. As a result of an international networking system, countries affect each other's economy. Illegal money transactions increase the gap between different classes of incomes. Governments cannot collect taxes from these illegal sources of income. Consequently, corruption increases.

Some bank offerings could attract money launderers, notably:

- A wide range of services and access to wider financial systems.
- International connections and facilities.
- Accessibility through networks. (Kumar, 2009)

A wide range of services and access to wider financial systems

A wide range of services and access to wider financial systems refer to the activity of controlling money transactions.

The Money-Laundering Cycle

Figure1.1 **The money-laundering cycle**

Source: UNODC (United Nations Office on Drugs and Crime) https://www.unodc.org/unodc/en/money-laundering/laundrycycle.html

Managing money laundering activities are difficult when financial activities increase and become complex.

International connections and facilities

International connections and facilities refer to the transfer of the funds. In addition, international connections make tracing money transactions difficult after the funds are transferred from one financial institution to another.

Accessibility through networks

International networks make money transfers easier.

Financing Terrorist Activities

The terrorism in the Southeast Asia and the financial sources behind the terrorist groups are mentioned by the authors. The authors also state that Southeast Asia has been a home for terrorist groups for decades. Islamic groups focus on religious and domestic issues such as adoption of Islamic law within Southeast Asia. The militant groups like Al Qaeda in the Southeast Asia are against globalization and America's increasing power in some countries like Iraq and Afghanistan. The authors argue that the militant groups in Southeast Asia are also trying to collaborate with other Muslim groups within the region to increase their financial power. Governments of Southeast Asia play a significant role in enforcing social discipline. The law and its penal sanctions could decrease terrorist activities if the governments of Southeast Asia apply them. (Vaughn et al., 2008)

Giraldo and Trinkunas explore the relation between terrorist activities and terrorism financing. The authors discuss various ways to finance terrorism by transferring the 'dirty money' (a term for illegally acquired funds) from one source to another. The writers also explore terrorist financing activities in different regions such as Arabia, Europe, East Africa, Southeast Asia, and South America. The authors also suggest developing a comparative perspective on the topic, possible solutions, and governments of Arabia, Europe, East Africa, Southeast Asia, and United States of America (USA)'s responses. For instance, after the attack of September 2001, the

USA government strengthened the anti-money laundering policies with the implementation of the Patriot Act (Giraldo and Trinkunas, 2007). As a result of the strict money laundering regulations within the Patriot Act in the USA, 'dirty money' activities have decreased. However, USA's strict policy about money laundering affects other regions. Terrorism funds and money-laundering activities increased in Europe as result of USA's Patriot Act (Giraldo and Trinkunas, 2007).

Financial Action Task Force (FATF) is an international standard setter for combating money laundering and terrorist financing (Borekci and Erol, 2011). The authors mention that Turkey's current situation has improved as a result of following FATF measures for combating money laundering and terrorist financing.

MASAK, the Turkey's Financial Crimes Investigation Board, explores preventing money laundering and terrorist financing in its Suspicious Transactions Guideline, published on the IBA Anti-Money Laundering Forum's website.[3] This website provides information about increasing the awareness and the importance of diagnosing money laundering actions and establishing anti-money laundering regulations. The website is a guideline for financial institutions and banks to improve their anti-money laundering action plans by providing information on different suspicious transaction types such as detecting abnormal money increases in a person's bank account, large cash movements from one bank account to another, or making payments to the same bank account by people without reasonable explanations (MASAK, 2011). MASAK also provides the authorized information and legal regulations for financial organizations to diagnose money-laundering issues. The legislation of terrorist financing and laundering proceeds of crime is analyzed from both national and international points of view (MASAK, 2011). National and international laws and regulations of terrorist financing and money-laundering help employees working in financial institutions be aware of the steps they need to follow to prevent Money-Laundering Activities (MLAs). For instance, national regulations include exchanging customer identifications with other institutions and periodically reporting the activities to presidency or the examiners (MASAK, 2011).

---

[3]http://www.anti-moneylaundering.org/

Corruption is a problem that financial institutions are dealing with. Understanding the nature of anti-corruption and the effects of corruption are vital information for the members of financial organizations to prevent it. Corruption has an effect on economic development projects, international business transactions, and government procurement activities (Olsen, 2010). Financial institutions could apply a compliance strategy to prevent the negative effects of corruption within organizations.

An effective compliance program includes corporate code of conduct, training and communication, compliance monitoring, auditing, reporting, and responding. Olsen provides the information about United States of America's government's effort to combat global corruption. He explores the subjects of nongovernment and world trade organizations, global forum on fighting corruption, international financial institutions, international chamber of commerce, transparency international, global corporate governance forum, the role of civil society, and the emerging markets to indicate the attempt of USA government's fight against global fraud.

Tracking the flow of the money in the globalized world is difficult for financial institutions. The international regulations for tracking money traffic are significant (Jojarth, 2009). Jojarth's book is a guideline that describes different ways of global money trafficking. The author discusses money laundering, narcotic drug trafficking, trading in small arms and light weapons, and diamonds as subjects of illegal money resources. The author mentions the importance of the Vienna Convention regarding money laundering. The Vienna Convention requires that countries provide the mutual legal guidance for international corporations to fight drug trafficking. Jojarth also examines the costs and benefits of the implementation of international drug control policies. The Vienna Convention Commission has policies for other types of crime and anti-money laundering, like the Financial Action Task Force (FATF), which was established for strengthening the efforts tracing the flow of funds of the member countries'. Jojarth argues that FATF and its 40 recommendations are the most important anti-money laundering initiatives available presently to financial institutions.

Money laundering is not always considered as harmful in some countries (Alexander, 2007). Money laundering could benefit some countries.

Jojarth mainly focuses on three areas: capital flight, avoidance of financial embargoes, and the investment of the earnings of corruption in a secure financial system. Jojarth discusses the position of the European Union (EU) toward money laundering. He describes ways of dealing with money laundering and its effect on financial institutions. Jojarth's book is a useful source of information for developing a new model of MLA enforcement to correct some issues that need to be addressed in anti-money laundering legislation.

'The Organization for Economic Cooperation and Development (OECD), the forum in which the governments of 30[4] democracies work together, deals with the social, economic, and environmental issues that arise from globalization' (Aiolfi, Dobovcek, Klemencic, Lebeaux, Ledergerber, Loo, Moehrenshlager, Pontifex, Savran, Uriarte and Zudova, 2008). The representatives of 30 governments also discuss different aspects of countries and regions dealing with money laundering activities. This article contains specific recommendations and policies about anti-corruption processes for each country in Eastern Europe and Central Asia.

Terrorism financing has a close relationship with money laundering. Terrorist groups aim to legalize or launder their 'dirty money'. To succeed, terrorist groups need to be able to raise funds and access to those funds to operate (Lormel, 2007). Lormel describes terrorist groups 'operations, purposes, and financial resources. He also discusses the relation between terrorist activities and its funding methods. Developing and applying detective and preventive strategies are vital for financial organizations to prevent money laundering. Lormel's article provides information about terrorist groups' funding capacities and mechanisms in their fundraising and operations.

Technology is necessary for financial organizations to work efficiently (Demetis, 2010). Demetis highlights the importance of technology in financial institutions while applying anti-money laundering policies. In addition, he mentions the most important initiatives that affected anti-money laundering (AML). The Vienna Convention, the Financial Action Task Force (FATF), the United Nations (UN) Convention,

---

[4]OECD is comprised of 35 countries as of August, 2016. http://www.oecd.org/internet/broadband-statistics-update.htm

and the Basel Committee have proposed and developed policies on anti-money laundering.

The 'Know Your Customer '(KYC) procedures play a vital role in protecting the reliability of the banking system and reducing the probability of banks becoming an instrument for money laundering, terrorist financing, and further illegitimate activities.

Terrorist financing causes various problems around the world (Koh, 2006). For that reason, international standards have been accepted and implemented by a number of countries for preventing financing terrorism. Koh examines the evolution and implementation of international standards against the terrorism financing. He includes examining and implementing the international standards of anti-terrorism financing by organizations like the FATF and the Basel Committee.

Risk assessment methods and mobile money services are important for money laundering and terrorist financing (Solin and Zerzan, 2010). Solin and Zerzan indicate that a risk assessment method has three main steps.

- Understanding the mobile money service
- Identifying Money Laundering and Terrorist Financing (ML/TF) vulnerabilities of the particular service
- Identifying how criminals could exploit these vulnerabilities.

Financial institution customers in developing countries can use mobile services to help prevent ML/TF activities. The Financial Action Task Force's (FATF)guideline suggests a risk assessment method to follow.

Trading activities are one of the oldest ways launderers use to move the money from one country to another. The guideline discusses money laundering and terrorist financing within the perspective of trading, and import-export activities (Zdanowicz, 2004). Zdanowicz examines the relation between transferring funds from the USA to other countries and terrorist activities within the guidance of data published by the Trade Research Institute.

Money laundering and terrorist financing has similarities and differences (Roberge, 2007). Money laundering is about protecting the income without following the law, whereas terrorist financing intends to support terrorist groups. Roberge's article presents targeted strategies for both illegal activities. Policies and regulations related with preventing money laundering mainly focus on financial services sector. On the other hand, terrorist groups are funding their groups with laundered money. The author indicates how money laundering and terrorist financing activities affect each other.

One of the most important ways financial institutions can fight money laundering is by knowing the customer (Low Kim Cheng, 2010). 'Knowing the customer' (KYC) means identifying the customer and the customer's business. The author indicates that knowing the customer is vital to knowing his or her needs. To prevent money laundering, employees in financial institutions should ask, check, and monitor the transactions of a customer. The author discusses the importance of screening customers.

Tracking and record-keeping are vital to prevent money laundering in financial institutions (Reider-Gordon, 2011). The author discusses worldwide and legal anti-money laundering developments including policies and enforcement actions in 2010. Employees in financial institutions need to be aware of the methods to combat terrorist financing. However, implementing methods to prevent money laundering activities within the financial institutions is difficult. In this research, the author explores implementation strategies of anti-money laundering applications.

Money laundering is an international problem. Implementing traditional methods to prevent money laundering in financial systems require important human resource effort and time (Le-Khac, Markos and Ketchadi, 2009). The author discusses an approach to improve the performance of data mining-based- solution for money laundering.

The effects of fighting against terrorism in financial institutions are different on society and individuals (Vlacek, 2007). A relation between individuals' liberty and security needs to be considered. Personal privacy and liberty arises from a surveillance of financial transactions to combat terrorist financing. Vlacek describes people banking experiences since 2001. After 2001, the requirement for Know Your Customer (KYC) became vital in the banking sector. KYC caused some problems for some recent immigrants concealing their finances from authorities. The author argues that the solution of the European Union is 'One-size-fits-All', means applying the same money laundering policies in the ECC.

Laws and regulations are developed for fighting corruption and fraud. However, some developing countries fail to apply anti-money laundering applications (Sharman and Chaikin, 2009). The authors examine the reasons and benefits of using anti-money laundering (AMLs) systems for anti-corruption purposes. They argue that applying anti-money laundering systems is logical in the standards for each cost of the former. They discuss how AML systems could expand the anti-corruption efforts, and they the importance of 'ownership' in applying AML applications in developing countries.

Detecting the action of money laundering is as important as reporting the action and applying anti-money laundering applications in financial organizations (Yang and Wei, 2010). The authors focus on three detection methods:

- Deviations in trading volume and frequency
- Unusual payments to or receipts from a typical trade partner, and
- The number of times a specific digit occurs in a particular position in numbers to detect financial fraud.

The authors also design an approach for detecting possible fraud and money laundering.

Governments have a significant role to stop terrorist financing activities (Lo, 2002). Lo discusses governments' responsibilities to combat terrorist financing. The mixture of tougher legislation, enforcement, and increased international cooperation of governments can be effective to fight against terrorist financing. The author also mentions Financial Action Task Force's (FATF) invitations and recommendations to other countries about joining the force to combat terrorist financing.

Terrorist groups are mostly established in the Middle East. The scale of those terrorist groups can be large or small (Rudner, 2010). Rudner focuses on large-scale terrorist groups that include a variety of networks within them. Rudner describes terrorist groups' resource requirements, and the role of military, media, enterprises, and underground networks for the groups' operational activities.

The procedures to avoid money laundering and terrorism financing in financial sector are vital in every country. To prevent money laundering and terrorism financing, private and public sector have different roles in implementation of protective procedures (Gordon, 2011). Gordon suggests that instead of private sector, governments of each country should take the responsibility of deciding whether the clients of financial institutions are money launderers or terrorists. Gordon presents information on how to prevent money laundering, the roles of the private sector, government's role to prevent money laundering, and terrorism financing, effectiveness of the current system, and successes and failures in private sector's role.

Anti-Money laundering policies and crime rates have a close relationship (Ferwerda, 2009). Ferwerda argues that the crime rates decrease as the anti-money laundering policies become stricter. However, implementing the policies in countries with high corruption levels is difficult. From the author's point of view, corruption affects money laundering in two different ways. Some degree of corruption attracts money laundering whereas some level of corruption decreases MLAs by increasing the risk of money launderers to lose their funds. According to the article, the development level of a country affects the success of implementing anti-money laundering policies.

Globalization has an effect on money laundering types. Money launderers find an alternative system - the trade-based money laundering that operates outside the financial systems (McSkimming, 2010). McSkimming observes that the policies to prevent trade-base money laundering are not successful because monitoring the activity is difficult. The author also adds that even if monitoring the data is possible, the application of policies would still be unsuccessful when the current system has major flaws. In this article, the writer also discusses the flaws of the system.

Transparency is the key to a successful global financial system (Baker, 2010). Financial institutions need to take several steps to fix the global economy. The first step is to eliminate secrecy of ownership. Determining the beneficial owners of the non-individual accounts, would protect the financial institutions from the unknown owners and money launderers. The second step is to report cross-border financial institutions' and multinational corporations' results on a country-by-country basis. The third step is to exchange tax information across the borders automatically. The final step is forbidding businesses to maintain two different sets of accounts. These steps are maintained to protect the financial institutions and businesses from illegal activities.

The use of Internet in business is important. Electronic money transferring is an opportunity for money launderers (Morris-Cotterill, 1999). Money launderers can send a message to hide, invest, or move the money via electronic money transferring systems. Internet banking systems are more efficient than traditional banking systems for financial funds transfer. This author discusses the method that money launderers use within the Internet banking systems.

Canadian anti-terrorism financing regulations have two components (Annand, 2011). The first is an amendment to the Criminal Code of Canada that includes the subjects of terrorist financing and related activities in the criminal code. The second includes the Proceeds of Crime Act that involves the money laundering and terrorist financing act. Annand discusses the success of Canada's current legal system on preventing terrorist financing by analyzing its negative and positive aspects. The author uses cost and benefit analysis to indicate the efficiency of anti-money laundering regulations of the existing legal system.

International businesses adopt anti-money laundering and combat terrorism financing applications by including reporting suspicious activities and knowing and identifying customers to protect their businesses from money laundering and terrorism financing (Delston and Walls, 2009). The authors describe trade-based money laundering and its requirements, Financial Action Task Force's (FATF) 40 requirements and implications for financial institutions including exporters, importers, and other traders.

European Union (EU) has some approaches to prevent money laundering and terrorist financing (Tavares and Thomas, 2010). Members of the EU need to apply the regulations imposed by the EU Commission. The authors measure money laundering at the European level. The authors also examine the statistical data between EU member countries and Suspicious Transaction Reports (STRs). The authors also observe and explain the reasons behind the difference in STRs for each country.

Financial Transactions and Reports Analysis Centre of Canada has recent (2016) information and developments about anti- money laundering regulations for financial institutions and the public.[5]

'General public and financial institutions should be aware of money laundering methods to chase dirty money' (Reuter and Truman, 2004). Knowing the methods and results of the crime has a relation with the crime's effect on macro and micro economy of a country. The authors also examine the prevention and enforcement methods of the crime.

'Money laundering can have devastating economic consequences' (Quirk, 1997). Fighting against money laundering is vital for all countries to prevent the negative effects of the crime. The author observes various ways of money laundering and problems that arise from it. Policy implications are significant for anti-money laundering efforts. The author also examines the importance of exchange controls, statistical reporting, and tax collection.

Yen (2005) examines the cost and benefit relation of anti-money laundering regulations. The author observes the efficiency of the regulations when costs of applying them change. He also compares the U. K with the USA, Italy, Germany, and France. The costs of applying AML applications vary in each country. The authors also observe people's perceptions on how the regulations are effective to prevent money laundering activities.

Rietbroek explores the significance of technology in money laundering methods. Launderers take advantage of the technology to launder dirty money. The main reason for launderers to choose digital system is the weakness in financial systems' regulations. As digital system improves the governments of countries have difficulties in adapting new technologies because of their limited budgets.

---

[5] Please note that you have a transition period of one year (June 30, 2016 to June 30, 2017) to adopt new methods to ascertain the identity of clients. http://www.fintrac .gc.ca/intro-eng.asp

CHAPTER 2

Money Laundering Methods

Money laundering is a process to conceal the illegal activity and present it as legal. The profits obtained with an illegal way by criminals are maintained from different ways. Some actions behind the illegal activity considered MLA contraventions include:

- Assets' exchange or transfer with hiding or dissimulating of the illegal source to avoid judgment and punishment,
- Hiding or dissimulating the origin of the place, circulation, property, or rights of the assets,
- Having the knowledge of the origin of the assets' funds, using and storing, is obtained by the illegal proceeds.

Criminals have various methods to launder dirty money obtained by illegal activities.

Structuring (Smurfing)

Launderers' initial desire is to enter cash into the financial system. To maintain their aim of cash entrance, launderers would prefer to transport capital to another country. The country they prefer is the one where detecting and reporting large cash transactions to the authorities within the financial institutions is less controlled. Structuring is performing of varying a financial transaction to prevent reporting obligations by law such as Bank Secrecy Act. The definition of smurfing is mentioned by Financial Transactions and Reports Analysis of Canada as, 'the act of using runners to perform multiple financial transactions to avoid the currency reporting requirements'. The structuring activity includes cash deposits which each is less than the minimum cash reporting obligations. According to Bank Secrecy Act, the regulation for Canada is as follows: 'For the purposes of reporting the importation or exportation of currency or monetary instruments of a certain value under subsection 12(1) of the Act, the prescribed value is $10,000'. This regulation is accepted by European and North American countries including USA, Canada, and Turkey.

Offshore Centers and Shell Corporations

Offshore centers and free zones have the advantage for money launderers in banking secrecy act, taxing, and its legal immunities.

Shell corporations could build to launder money as well. These organizations only exist on paper and perform undersized businesses or no businesses at all. Launderers both use offshore zones and shell corporations to launder money in layers easily. For instance, money launderers can buy real estate and assets and sell them to one's own shell corporation. After that, they can pass the funds with the original price to a third party corporation that has no relationship with the launderers.

Casinos and Other Gambling Alternatives

Casino and Other Gambling alternatives maintain an approachable way for launderers to move money from one source to another. Clients in casinos purchase chips with cash. During or after the gambling, the chips of the customers' are traded in for a check by the casino.

Lottery and horse racing also can be considered as gambling. 'Winning tickets bought at a slight premium, allowing the winner to collect money without tax liability and enabling the launderer to collect a check from the track' (Reuter,. 2004). Lotteries are similar to horse tracks in the way of purchasing the winning tickets from the winners at the time they arrive to the lottery offices to collect their money. As an example given in FATF's website in 2002, a professional gambler who had the checks for the winnings opened 14 different bank accounts under 10 different third party identities. Those identities mostly belonged to robbers and other criminals with different crimes.

Banking Transactions

The most difficult stages for criminals to launder money could be listed as:

- Entering cash to the bank
- Transferring money into and out from the financial institutions
- Taking the cash over the borderline

These activities are maintained within the financial institutions by launderers. Therefore, criminals need to manage the process well to deceive bank employees or managers that the source of the money is legal. (See Figure 2.1. Money Laundering Activities in Money Laundering Stages)

The banks are chosen as the prime money laundering settings. The reason is related with banks' ability to transfer the capital or generated assets in large quantities in a short time to the overseas countries. The speed is vital for the money launderers. Criminals' urgent motivation is to move as soon as possible. By the help of using the three stages of money

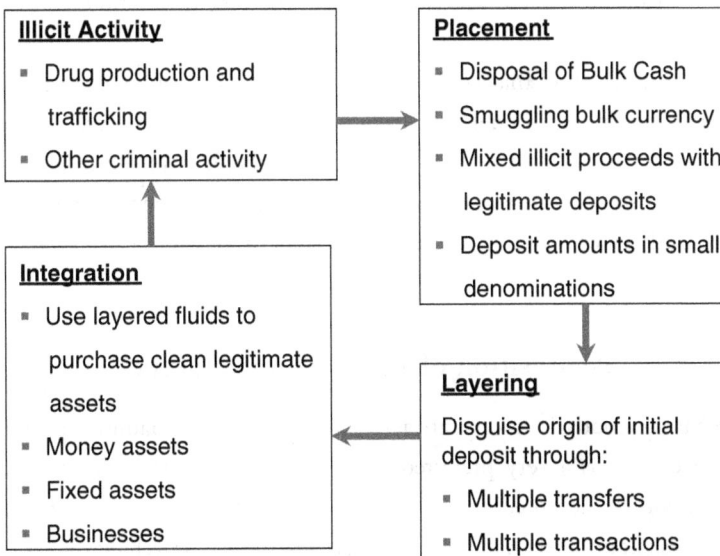

Figure 2.1. **Money Laundering Activities in Money Laundering Stages**

Source: BCM Training programme- in Turkey 2005

laundering, placement, layering, and integration, money launderers can easily make illegal evidences disappear. Launderers can also launder money with using alternative methods like:

- Internet banking,
- False identification, and
- Credit card payments

Internet banking is an easy way to collect funds. Financial institutions have established strict regulations to prevent fraud within financial systems. However, customers can transfer large quantities of money easily. The clients could transfer funds to domestic or external accounts as greatly as they want. However, the repetition of money transfers could make tracking difficult. To control those types of activities, employees in financial institutions should know the customers' account history and their businesses well.

False identification of customers could mislead financial institutions and create an easier environment for laundering money. The forms of false identification could also include fake accounts, debit and credit capacities, and assets.

Another method that launders can achieve their goals is using credit cards. A credit card holder can make large payments with a credit card to a bank. Regarding to this transaction, the bank pays the difference between the loan of the customer and the received payment by a check. The launderer who also is the credit card holder receives the clean money and deposits it into the cash.

Acquisition of Property and Assets

Purchasing goods is a very attractive field for money launderers. For instance, gold is a very preferred element by launderers because of its internationally accepted store value and moving availabilities through countries. Launderers can also purchase real estate or vehicles abroad. Criminals accomplish laundering activities by third parties or dealers. Dealers purchase the goods launderers sell and resell the received goods to launderers.

Technology

Technology is one of the methods that launderers chose to manipulate the flow of the money. Criminals would always search for a weakness of the AML procedures and systems in financial institutions. Digital AML regulations are one of the financial institutions' weaknesses. Some methods that launderers take advantage of in technology are as follows:

- Digital Smurfing:

Launderers mostly prefer to transfer dirty money where financial institutions are not strict about reporting large cash deposits to the authorities. 'The type of activity that involves large fund transfers is called 'Bulk cash smuggling" (Rietbroek, 2009). Bulk cash smuggling is a challenge because the value of the smuggled products such as drugs, is heavier than the transferred cash itself. For instance, launderers use vehicles to transport drugs as a return for their large cash transfers. Therefore, cash money needs to be deposited in bank accounts and converted into a electronic funds.

- Digital Currency Accounts:

Digital Currency Accounts create an opportunity for launderers to move dirty money across countries. Digital currencies include the materials with internationally accepted values such as gold or silver. These types of accounts can be opened online. The only difference between digital precious metal accounts and bank accounts is their types of funds. In digital metal accounts funds are held in valuable metals, whereas most bank accounts are held in various currencies. Use of the digital currency method is mostly preferred by launderers because of the vastly pervasive digital currency industry. Another reason for launderers' attention on the digital currency account is the minimal customer identification process. Unlike traditional bank accounts, digital currency accounts can be funded anonymously. In addition, these accounts allow individuals to carry out multiple digital currency transactions over a short time. ATM's are available to launderers around the world when the currency funds can be converted and transferred to prepaid cards.

Rietbroek (2009) describes various ways to avoid such money laundering methods. However, she adds that some countries' government agencies are often short of funds to follow new trends and techniques and act too slowly. Besides government agencies, financial institutions face additional expenses to improve their detecting and monitoring methods to prevent money laundering crimes arise from the use of technology.

CHAPTER 3

Money Laundering Detection Methods

Money laundering is a dynamic process. It involves a circulation of money or fund transfers in and out of a country to legalize the source of those funds. Some measures to decrease the circumvention of this form of illegal activity include:

- Deviations in trading volume and frequency,
- Unusual payments and receipts from an unusual trade partner, and
- Financial Fraud which is known as Benford's Law, based on the numbers of times a specific digit occurs in a particular position in numbers to detect financial fraud (Yang and Wei, 2010).

Many applications and reporting regulations are published by anti-money laundering institutions for financial organizations or public to collaborate with AML procedures. These procedures and models have resulted in stopping some dynamic money laundering activities. However, applying each detection model at the same time is difficult because of the amount of information involved.

Trading volume and frequency could be measured by Transaction Assessment as a result of applying a detection model that observes Normal Behavior Patterns.[1] According to that model, the technique is to evaluate

---

[1]Typically the anomalous items will translate to some kind of problem such as bank fraud, a structural defect, medical problems or errors in a text. Anomalies are also referred to as outliers, novelties, noise, deviations and exceptions.

the information with the unusual (outlier) behavioral pattern in the same data set. For example,

- If monthly trading volume and frequency do not match with the Normal Behavior Pattern (NBP), the targeting company would be suspicious, which means that the targeted business is not stable and could involve money laundering activities.

Every company in a stable business has a certain capacity and content. The Trade Correlation Test conformity requires saving all the receipts and payments received from the buyers and suppliers that the company had relation with. With this method, companies may save themselves from involvement in money laundering activities. To achieve that objective, they need to provide evidence of their receipts and payments matching the scope and subject of their businesses.

The Financial Fraud Detection method is based on Benford's Law[2] used to identify accounting capabilities, fraud, and profit manipulations in corporations. The law is not very functional for individuals because of its structure. The law's structure is based on evaluating the numbers on an income statement of a company. The account needs to involve money received from falsified entries such as forged financial statements or taxes. Cash flow, total assets, account receivables and payables, and the balance sheet include significant data allowing to examine the financial information of a company.

Some weaknesses of these techniques result when each of them is applied only individually in a corporate organization:

- Transaction Assessment would not be successful when the corporate firm's data is close to the targeted data in a same company.

---

[2]Benford's Law (in mathematics) is the principle that in any large, randomly produced set of natural numbers, such as tables of logarithms or corporate sales statistics, around 30 percent will begin with the digit 1, 18 percent with 2, and so on, with the smallest percentage beginning with 9. The law is applied in analyzing the validity of statistics and financial records.

- The Trade Correlation Test is a very effective method to examine if the company's trading status is matching with its business scope. However, this detection strategy could not verify whether the company is related with money laundering activities or not.
- Finally, the Fraud Detection method is related only with some particular accounts where fraud might exist. These accounts require detailed analyses by the authorities to find money laundering activities within.

Applying all these methods together is called the 'Multiple Detections Approach (MDA)' (Yang and Wei, 2010). MDA is a method to reduce the weaknesses of these three methods when applied individually. Moreover, a money laundering activity may not be detected with only one of these three detection methods. At this point, MDA is the best approach to detect fraud in financial institutions. If a company fails all three of these detection methods, the organization is suspected of money laundering activities.

In addition to the detection methods above, other techniques are used in trading (export and import) activities of financial organizations to detect money laundering and terrorism financing movements. Some different conditions are listed as follows:

1. Overvalued Import Transactions

The value of an imported product is more than its worth and the exporter abroad pays inflated price for the product. As a result, the possession is transferred from the domestic importer to the foreign exporter. The deal is not profitable for the importer. However, if both sides of the business transaction are partners they both share the profit. These kinds of over-priced import transactions may cause three types of crimes:

- Customs Fraud, Income Tax Evasion, and Money Laundering (Zdanowicz, 2004).

In addition, the exporter, who receives the money from the domestic importer, might be a member of a terrorist organization and use the fund to serve that purpose. In that case, the transactions would take the form as presented in the example below:

- A criminal desires to launder $1 million through an exporter as a business partner to a foreign country. The steps he would follow would be:
  - The exporter purchases 10,000 products paying $0.10 for each or $1,000 in total.
  - The exporter exports 10,000 overpriced products to the domestic importer for $100 each. The invoice of the transaction is worth $1,000,000.
  - The domestic importer pays $1 million for those 10,000 products (originally worth $1,000)
  - As a result, the domestic importer launders $1 million to a foreign country through the transaction including the original cost of the products at $1,000

2. Undervalued Export Transactions

Another method that criminals choose to launder money to a foreign country is undervalued export transactions.

The domestic exporter purchases products at its market price. These products are shipped to the foreign importer for undervalued prices (below products' market prices). The importer receives the products below their market value and sells them at their original market prices to make a profit.

According to the research of Zdanowicz, (a Finance professor at Florida University and previous director of the Center for Banking and Financial Institutions, as well as a consultant to the U. S. Department of Justice on transfer pricing and money laundering), terrorist and launderers prefer this method as the most common technique for laundering money out of the United States. Some of the reasons behind the preference of undervalued export transactions are:

- Most governments do not effectively monitor their export transactions, and
- Criminals do not use financial institutions for their transactions because government agencies monitor them.

Money Laundering and the Combat with Terrorism Financing (CTF)

After the attack on the Twin Towers on September 11, 2001, the threat of terrorist activities became more important. The unfortunate event increased the awareness of people on terrorism and their financing activities. Terrorist groups achieve their illegal activities with the support of their financial sources. The members of terrorist groups aim to launder their financial source of funds to use them for future illegal and criminal activities. The terrorist organizations require financial support to maintain their growth and profit.

MASAK (The Financial Crimes Investigation Board of Turkey) introduced some measures to curtail terrorism financing by expanding its Suspicious Transactions list and bettert protect financial organizations from theterrorist financing. According to the 2009 Turkish Criminal Law No. 5237, the penalties for crimes of terrorism financing and money laundering are as follows:

- A person who conceals the source of an income gained from a crime can be sentenced to prison from 3 to 7 years, and a person who transfer the money gained from an illegal activity could end up 6 months in prison.
- A person who was not involved the crime but obtains or uses the proceeds of the crime could be sentenced from 2 to 5 years to prison.
- If the crime is committed during on duty by a professional or a public officer, the penalty could increase by one half.
- The penalty could be doubled when the crime is performed in an organization created to committing a crime.
- A person who directly secures the financial assets by reporting the crime to the related authorities before it actuates will not be punished.

'Criminal organizations and terrorist groups share some similar traits in their organizational structure and dangers they pose to society' (Roberge, 2007). Criminal organizations plan their activities for profit when terrorist groups plan their actions for political objectives. However, terrorist groups do not only aim to use their funds for acts of terror. Terrorist organizations may also fund organized and militant groups with political objectives.

Terrorism is a very debatable subject. It can also refer to people fighting for their freedom and independence. For that reason, differentiating the terms 'guerilla warfare' from 'terrorism' by examining their activities is difficult. Some terrorist organizations offer welfare-type of services and some business branches that include political, social, and terror activities. Some governments decrease money laundering and terrorist financing activities by shutting down the charity organizations which might be involved in illegal activities.

Profit and politically focused organizations are also difficult to distinguish. However, they may be connected in some situations. Politically focused groups need funds to continue their activities when they collaborate with other organizations to gain access to illegal sources of funds. On the other hand, profit based organization are not necessarily collaborating with politically focused groups.

Besides organizations, individuals can also support terrorist groups or politically focused organizations. I Individuals or organizations may provide funds to the terror groups voluntarily or under threat. For instance, Pickert states that the Tamil Tigers of Sri Lanka is one of the most organized, brutal, and effective terrorist groups in the world. The members of the group fight for their freedom to separate from Sri Lanka. The group members continue their activities and receive their funds mostly from drug smuggling and robberies. Members of Tamil Tigers also threats people to fund their activities.

Extortion is a generally preferred method by terrorists, especially in drug smuggling. The Washington Post published in 2012 an article about a Canadian who admitted trying to help the members of, the Tamil Tigers, considered a terror organization in Canada. He admitted that he provided $22,000 worth of material in support of the terrorist organization in February of that year.

Terrorism also can be financed by states such as Libya and Iran. Roberge states that Saudi Arabia and some countries in the Middle Eastern Region transferred many times funds to terrorist groups like Al Qaeda and Osama Bin Laden.

Money laundering and terrorist financing activities also affect international financial system in different ways. Money laundering decreases the financial stability and harms the reputation of legitimate organizations when terrorism activities can harm the financial system.

Money launderers can transfer and receive the dirty-money several times by using the same financial institutions to launder the funds.

The use of offshore centers is another efficient way to launder money. Money launderers prefer offshore services, where financial services are offered to non-residents as well as residents, especially in layering stages where they aim to conceal the source of the money. Terrorist organizations also prefer to operate in places where authority is deficient, like in some offshore centers.

Terrorism financing does not require 'placement, layering, and integration stages' as money laundering does. According to Zen, the source of terrorism financing may not be illegal so it does not need to be laundered to integrate into the economy. Only the layering stage could be common in both illegal activities to conceal the source of the money.

CHAPTER 4

Effects of Money Laundering on the Macro Economy

Money laundering has significant effects on a country's macro economy. The effect can be direct or indirect.

Direct effect of money laundering on economy could be:

- Tax Evasion,
- Low-quality investments, and
- Decrease or stability in a country's economic growth.

Laundered money would enter the economy with no official records, thereby evading taxes. Money launderers would not pay tax on their 'earnings'. As a result, economic growth of the country will suffer. Investments would decrease because of the lack of economic growth stability. Investors prefer more profitable countries to meet their earnings expectations.

Money laundering can also affect indirectly the macro economy. For example, some banking transactions involve multiple sides including domestic and abroad. These activities can be completely legal. However, financial institutions are less likely to prefer these transactions because its structure makes money laundering possible.

Money laundering involves numerous economic activities within a country. Studies of macroeconomists claim that underground economy, and profitable activities unreported for evading tax, could be measured by measuring money laundering activities in a country. Indeed, if taxes are high in a country, the attempts for evading taxes would also be high.

The 1980s research on that topic estimates that countries' underground economy sizes are represented with their GDP percentage as follows:

- Australia: 4%-12%
- Italy: 10%-33%
- Germany: 2%-11%
- Japan: 4%-15%
- United Kingdom: 1%-15%
- United States of America: 4%-33% (Quirk, 1997).

GDP represents the value of products and services provided in the market. Therefore, the countries above have developed underground economies related reflecting their currency and money demand. Quirk also states that in the 1980-90 period, increase in money laundering activities is related to a considerable drop in annual GDP growth rates.

From the financial markets' point of view, money is laundered as:

- **Smurfing**: Money is laundered by multiple cash transactions smaller than the maximum transferring cash transaction of a country that requires reporting.
- **Creating artificial invoices**: Money is laundered by false export and import invoices, L/C's (letter of credits), and custom declarations.
- **Trading**: Money is laundered by exchanging properties in and out of the country.
- **Parallel Credit Transactions**: Money is laundered by avoiding formal economy by purchasing legally marketed goods or services with dirty money.
- **Interbank wire transfers**: Money is laundered by the help of the employees of a financial institution. Bank officials can conceal the sources or the transactions' values. This illegal activity results in corruption in work places.
- **Imitating transactions**: Money is laundered by using company's trading opportunities to benefit the situation as concealing some illegal activities within the company.

Corruption and Money Laundering

According to the Economist (2001), corruption occurs more in private banking systems than in public systems. Clients in private financial institutions are mostly wealthy and prefer that their transactions occur in discreet conditions. Those clients seem to prefer banks asking fewer questions. Consequently, thia situation may generate more money laundering activities.

Offshore centers also create an opportunity of corruption and money laundering opportunities. According to the Economist (2001), as of 1998, there were 4,000 licensed offshore banks including:

- 44% in the Caribbean and Latin America,
- 28% in Europe,
- 18% in Asia,
- 10% in the Middle East and Africa.

The most difficult version of offshore banks to control money laundering activities is shell banks with no physical presence.

Corruption is the offering, providing, obtaining, and asking for directly or indirectly of anything with value to influence inappropriately the actions of another party.[1]

Corruption includes wider type of criminal activities than money laundering. However, money laundering activities are related to corruption and anti-money laundering activities can help preventing fraud.

Reasons to achieve AML regulations to fight corruption are as follows:

- International anti-corruption requires achieving international AML standards, and
- Application of those standards in both developing and developed countries. (Sharman, 2009).

---

[1]According to the Uniform Framework for Preventing and Combating Fraud and Corruption released in 2006 by The International Financial Institutions Anti-Corruption Task Force,

However, direct and indirect costs of AML applications could be high for underdeveloped countries to afford. In these countries, corruption is one of the most important methods for launderers.

Despite of AML systems' expenses, countries should adopt AML laws and regulations and international standards to prevent organized crime, drug smuggling, financing terrorism, and corruption activities.

Financial company managers should consider:

- **Monitoring**: Managers should inform employees about the document policies in financial institutions. Communicating in all levels of the workplace is vital for both financial institutions and employees to implement the strategies correctly. To achieve the perfect solution out of communication, managers should monitor the processes. Monitoring improves the quality of the work and keeps the employees ready for new policies and regulations.
- **Reducing the Risk**: Managers and directors of a company aim to reduce the risk of document retention by using technology such as: backing up e-mails daily, storing documents properly aligned with regulations, controlling the methods of recovering data, and improving data searching techniques.

According to 'Corporate and Criminal Fraud Accountability Act' criminal and civil penalties associated with artificial document protection are as follows:

- Knowing any damage, alteration, or falsification in federal research and bankruptcy could result in imprisonment of up to 20 years.
- Knowing and destruction of companies' audit records could result in imprisonment of up to 10 years.

CHAPTER 5

Suspicious Transaction Types

According to MASAK's website, suspicious transaction types are mentioned as follows:

- Circumstances of clients not willing to provide information about the transaction or themselves during the operation. Additional situations include providing inadequate or wrong information or documents and the purpose of the transaction to the relevant authorities or financial institutions. or cases when transactions do not meet its declared purposes.
- Establishing transactions by transferring large funds to countries with illegal activities such as; drug trafficking, smuggling, or terrorist financing. These large transactions could also be directed to offshore centers.
- Inactive bank accounts with large sums of money within and detecting unusual and high increases within these bank accounts.
- Large sums of money transfers by customers to different accounts and addresses than regular transfer accounts or addresses.
- Large sums of cash movements send by accounts from other countries to a customer with bad reputation, no definite business, and no business background.
- Large sums of money transfers to or from abroad with no reasonable explanation and requiring cash payment of electronic money transfers.

- There is more than one account of a customer and the funds within these accounts become large when they are combined. Not reporting the number of these transactions could lower number of transfers identified.
- Transferring money by variety of people and accounts to the same bank account with no rational information.
- Opening a deposit account for transferring money to banks abroad by people with small businesses that does not require a banking transaction in their countries. Moreover, transferring deposited cash with aiming to transport money into different bank accounts by reserving and holding the money within the account for a short time.
- Transferring money that are not maintained from commercial functions and making payments to people or organizations that are not related with the company or the person that has an account in the financial institution.
- Obtaining high loans and paying the credits with unpredicted ways with providing no information in a short time.
- Receiving loans in home country by presenting a bank account as a collateral in a foreign country under the conditions of:
  - Paying the credit abroad by transferring the deposited money from off shore banks overseas.
- Not providing information or a reasonable explanation about where to use or how to pay the loan when demanding credit.
- Transferring similar funds from or to other countries.
- Providing selling and acquiring orders for the accounts in future and stock markets aiming to achieve transactions with no reasonable purpose.
- Having two or more accounts, which are performing on the stock exchange, with similar transactions including regular profit and loss, belongs to one client.
- Different investors are sending money or their profits to the same account with the purpose of closing an account with a big loss.

- Transferring large sums of money on the date of accounts are opened.
- Brokers open various accounts to maintain same type of transactions to conceal money transaction movements.
- Suspecting that the funds in the accounts are related to terrorism activities, financing or purposes.

Some examples of cases related with such transactions in Turkey are described hereafter.

A Case of Money Laundering Resulting from Corruption

Gabriel, a Romanian resident, is working under a contract for a foreign company, SC Ltd, and has a high public position. The company had recently made an acquisition of a foreign company. After the acquisition the foreign company sends USD 1,020,000 using a foreign fund registered in a tax-free offshore centre.

SC Ltd transfers,

- USD 150,000 to the bank account in Hungary, and
- USD 300,000 to the bank account in Austria on the behalf of Gabriel's name.

On the same day of the fund transfers, SC Ltd transfers USD 570,000 from Romania to the bank in a foreign country under the name of 'Account 1' on behalf of a Romanian citizen (Gabriel). A few days later, Gabriel places USD 450,000 cash into the bank account 'Account 1' from his bank account in Romania. On the same day of the transaction he is also:

- Opens an account as 'Account 2' in a foreign country and transfers USD 420,000 to the new account from Romania,
- Opens an account as 'Account 3' in a foreign country and transfers USD 480,000 to the new account from Romania, and
- Carries out exchanges of USD 120,000 worth in cash.

On the next day, Gabriel performs the following transactions from 'Account 2':

- Transfer of USD 170,000 to a non-profit organization directed by his wife,
- Transfer of USD 210,000 to different accounts that belong to his relatives, and
- Transfer USD 40,000 into his credit card account.

On the same day, Gabriel, using 'Account 3' does the following transactions:

- Paying USD 110,000 of life insurance policies,
- Withdrawing USD 265,000 cash,
- Paying USD 35,000 education expenses to the same non-profit organization directed by his wife, and
- Transferring USD 70,000 to an auto dealer.

Managers in the banks of the foreign countries that have Account 1, Account 2, and Account 3 suspected the transactions of Gabriel to be fraudulent and report the issue. As a result, National Office for Combating and Preventing Money Laundering analysed the suspected transactions and reported to the authorities to examine the whole money route.

Suspicious Transaction Case 1

A cash transaction above USD 10,000 is performed by a client company. The manager of the bank has identified the transaction and reported the operation as suspicious. The account was opened on 2011-08-01. The suspicious transactions started as follows:

- The client company M receives wire transfers with the explanation of invoice payments and borrowings large sums from business partners.
- On the same day of the transaction, money is transferred to another account with the explanation of material costs by the authorized individual of the company.

- The transactions were both performed in one branch of the bank.
- The client M has increased his proceeds in the bank account to USD 339,000

As a result, the bank manager examined the transactions and found them suspicious. He reported the case to the AML director as suspicious.

Suspicious Transaction Case 2

A client deposits USD 62,000 cash to his bank account. The funds on the clients account have three months maturity. The client transfers money in two parts with the explanation that he is loaning funds to two different companies. Both of the transactions are completed before the time of their maturities with no valid explanations. The client does not have income and is in no stable economic condition. Furthermore, the client will not receive interest from his account because he took out funds before their maturity.

The account was opened in 2008 and the client has not updated any personal information since then. According to the bank's internal procedures, the bank employees were not requesting detailed information from their clients since 2010. The account was opened in 2008 so the personnel of the bank did not receive any kind of new information from the client. In 2010, bank employees started to collect data from its clients and received information about the suspected client. According to his identification, he was unemployed and has no additional income. The branch manager noticed the movements within the client's account and compared the transactions with his personal data. As a result, the transactions are reported as suspected to the authorities, AML directors.

After the managers updated the bank's inner procedures about 'know your customer (KYC)' policies, money laundering transactions became easier to detect and report.

This case illustrates how important internal regulations of the financial institutions can be.

According to the records of MASAK in 2009, the number of suspicious financial transactions which are reported to the Financial Action Task Force (FATF) has increased from 180 to 4,318 in the period of 2003 to 2008. The results represent a 24-fold increase for that period.

CHAPTER 6

Organizations Dealing with Money Laundering and Terrorist Financing

Criminals are interested in funding their activities and make profit out of their illegal activities. I Illegal activities might include fraud, drug and arm trafficking, money laundering, and terrorist financing. To prevent illegal activities, money-laundering and terrorist financing, different organizations, and conventions accept and implement international laws and regulations.

Financial Action Task Force (FATF)[1]

The most recognized organization FATF was established to prevent money-laundering activities.

The FATF was established by the G-7 (Group of 7 countries) Summit that was held in Paris 1989 (Borekci and Erol, 2011).

The FA Task Force is a policy making organization that develops procedures at national and international levels. According to Borekci and Erol, in 1990, the FATF introduced 40 recommendations which provided a comprehensive plan of action needed to fight against money

---

[1] The Financial Action Task Force (FATF) is an inter-governmental body established in 1989 by the Ministers of its Member jurisdictions. The objectives of the FATF are to set standards and promote effective implementation of legal, regulatory and operational measures for combating money laundering, terrorist financing and other related threats to the integrity of the international financial system. The FATF is therefore a "policy-making body" which works to generate the necessary political will to bring about national legislative and regulatory reforms in these areas. See: http://www.fatf-gafi.org/

laundering. Those recommendations became international set of standards. The FATF has updated its policies against money laundering and terrorist financing through the years. 'On 22 October 2004, the FATF has arranged the 40+9 recommendations which include additional 9 policies about terrorist financing' (Koh, 2006). According to the FATF's website, G-7 was formed in 1976, when Canada joined the group of six countries: France, Germany, Italy, Japan, United Kingdom, and United States.

The 40 Recommendations could be categorized in 4 groups,

- Legal Systems include the scope of the criminal offence of money laundering and provisional measures.
- Measures used by Financial and Non-financial Institutions include
  - financing,
  - customer care,
  - record-keeping,
  - Reporting suspicious transactions,
  - Measures to be taken with respect to countries that do not or inadequately fulfill the FATF Recommendations, and
  - Regulations and supervisions.
- Institutional and Other Measures in Systems include
  - Competent authorities, their powers, and resources
  - Transparency of legal people and arrangements
- International Cooperation includes mutual legal assistance and transportation and other forms of co-operation.

The FATF organization has 37 members (35 member jusrisdictions and 2 regional organisations) representing most major financial centres in all parts of the globe.

The organization is in close collaboration and cooperation with other international bodies involved in the AML/CTF area, in particular with the International Monetary Fund (IMF) and the World Bank (Borekci, 2011). The IMF and the World Bank are the vital organizations for the assessment and implementation of the FATF standards. The FATF also works with the Basel Committee on banking supervision and Organization for Economic Cooperation and Development (OECD).

Turkey's Mutual Evaluation Process of the Financial Action Task Force

The 40 Recommendations for AML/CTF (Combat terrorism financing) are applicable to all countries. The mutual evaluation process of the FATF requirements is an element for deciding if countries are in fulfillment with the recommendations of FATF or not.

Based on FATF, four possible ways of fulfillment for each recommendation include:

- **Largely compliant (LC):** The majority of the essential criteria are fulfilled with some minor shortcomings.
- **Partially compliant (PC):** Some actions are taken by the country and some of the essential criteria are fulfilled.
- **Non-compliant (NC):** The majority of the essential criteria are unfulfilled with some major shortcomings.
- **Not Applicable (N/A):** Because of the structural, legal, or institutional attributions of a country, a requirement or a part of a requirement does not accomplished.

The FATF Recommendations have core and key measures. Since 1991, Turkey has been a member of FATF. The final Mutual Evaluation Report (MER) has been estimated in 2007. According to the report including the core and key recommendations of FATF, Turkey's mutual evaluation is shown below (See the following Tables 6.1 and 6.2):

Table 6.1 FATF core and key recommendations

Rec	1	3	4	5	10	13	23	26	35	36	40	I	II	III	IV	V
Rating	PC	LC	LC	NC	C	PC	PC	LC	PC	LC	LC	PC	PC	PC	PC	PC

Source: ICRG, Report by the Europe/Eurasia Regional Review Group Co-Chairs, FATF/ICRG (2009)19, 30 September 2009, p: 96.

The explanation of the core and key recommendations is as follows:

Table 6.2 Explanations of Recommendations

Recommendation	Explanation	Rating
Legal System		
1	ML Offence	PC
3	Measures of Confiscation and Provision	LC
Preventive Measures		
4	Secrecy laws consistent with the Recommendations	LC
5	Customer due diligence	NC
10	Record Keeping	Compliant
13	Suspicious Transaction Reporting	PC
23	Regulation, Supervision, and Monitoring	PC
INSTITUTIONAL AND OTHER MEASURES		
26	The FIU (Financial Intelligence Units)	LC
INTERNATIONAL COOPERATION		
35	Conventions	PC
36	Mutual Legal Assistance	LC
40	Other Forms of Cooperation	LC
FIVE OUT OF NINE SPECIAL RECOMMENDATIONS (SR)		
SR, I	Implement UN (United Nation) Instruments	PC
SR, II	Criminalize Terrorist Financing	PC
SR, III	Freeze and Confiscate Terrorist Assets	PC
SR, IV	Suspicious Transaction Reporting	PC
SR, V	International Cooperation	PC

Source: ICRG, Report by the Europe/Eurasia Regional Review Group Co-Chairs, FATF/ICRG (2009)19, 30 September 2009

Shortages in those recommendations show the need of the need of serious measures in a country's AML/CTF system to reflect a stronger international financial system. According to the table above, for Turkey, the evaluation includes 9 PC and 1 NC out of 16 core and key recommendations.

In January 2010, MASAK, the Turkish Financial Crimes Investigation Board stated the need for the implementation of the AML/CTF system according to its 40 FATF recommendations and prepared an action plan. The Turkish government submitted a plan including standards and criteria of

- Criminalizing the financing of terrorism and associated money laundering (SR II), and
- Freezing and confiscating terrorist assets (SR III).

According to the ICRG (International Country Risk Guide) report, this action plan has been adopted and lead by the delegate prime minister and several authorities, including the Ministries of Justice, Interior, Foreign Affairs as well as MASAK.

European Union (EU) Money-Laundering Combat Directives

The EU has introduced a total of three directives to combat money laundering:

- A Council Directive in 1991,
- A Directive in 2001 of the European Parliament and Council, and
- A Directive in 2005 of the European Parliament and Council.

The directives deal with:

- The definition of AML,
- Specification of Categories of Financial Intermediaries,
- Obligations of these intermediaries,
- Explanation of these obligations,
- Identification of the Responsibilities of Public Authorities, and
- Control purposes.

The directives are vital for establishing the control for environment against money laundering and terrorist financing. The directives include four major criteria:

- Customer Identification (Know Your Customer)
  - Record Keeping
  - Suspicious Transactions, and
  - Reporting.

The third AML directive, adopted in 2005, is the most important one among the others with international approaches of preventing money-laundering activities, terrorist financing activities, and suspicious transaction reporting.

Turkey is a European Union candidate country. For that reason, the country will not be involved in this section. However, the organization has 28 countries as of July 2013[2], as follows:

- Austria,
- Belgium, Bulgaria,
- Cyprus, Czech Republic, Croatia
- Denmark,
- Estonia,
- Finland, France,
- Germany, Greece,
- Hungary,
- Ireland, Italy,
- Latvia, Lithuania, Luxemburg
- Malta,
- The Netherlands,
- Poland, Portugal,
- Romania,
- Slovakia, Slovenia, Spain, Sweden, and
- United Kingdom. [Brexit pending – 2016][3]

Figure 6.1 describes the European Financial Institutions: distribution by Country Reported figures above differ according to the countries' financial markets. The main reason for that variation emanates from the

---

[2]Source:https://europa.eu/european-union/about-eu/countries/member-countries_en

[3] **Brexit** is the forthcoming withdrawal of the United Kingdom (UK) from the European Union (EU). In the June 2016 referendum, 52% voted to leave the EU, leading into a complex separation process implying political and economic changes for the UK and other countries. As of August 2016, neither the timetable nor the terms for withdrawal have been established: in the meantime, the UK remains a full member of the European Union. The term "Brexit" is a portmanteau of the words "British" and "exit" https://en.wikipedia.org/wiki/Brexit

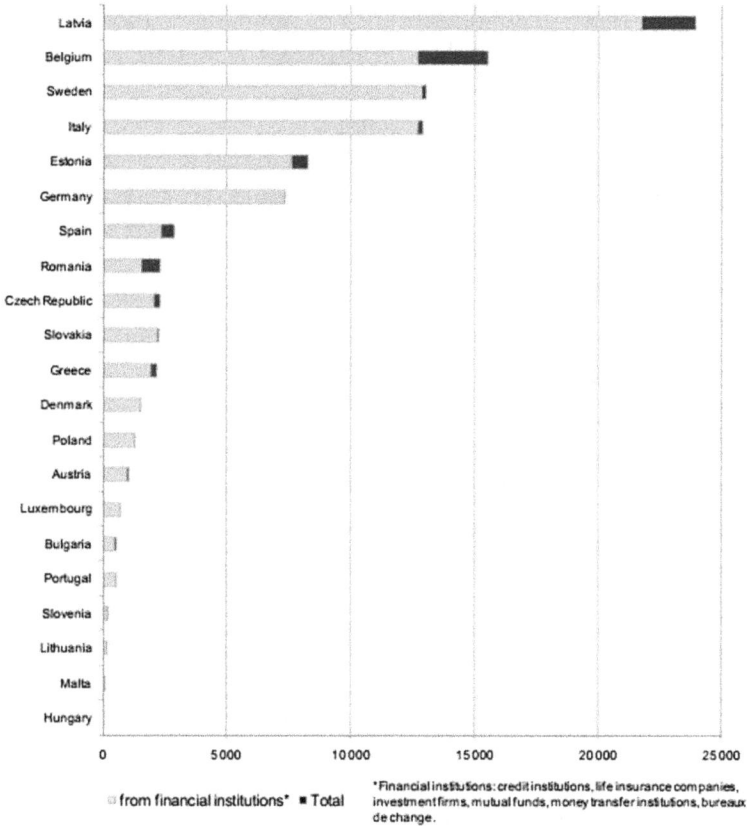

Figure 6.1 European Financial Institutions

Source: Eurostat

different counting rules and concepts within EU. The transaction processes are as follows:

- Financial Intelligence Units (FIUs) process transactions received in Suspicious Transaction Reports (STRs) as cases.
- The related cases are sent to the Law Enforcement Authorities.
- Some FIUs record and combine all related STRs as one case, when some FIUs count the STRs as the first case-opening.

For some EU members, the activities which might not be related to any monetary transaction, such as opening a bank account, could be interpreted as a Suspicious Activity Report (SAR). On the other hand, some EU members could send Unusual Transaction Reports (UTR) to the law enforcement authorities if those activities are found to be suspicious.

European Union's (EU) Action Plan to Fight Against Terrorist Funding

The European Union has adopted its fourth directive on May 20th, 2015. Its main goal is to prevent the EU financial system from being used for money laundering and terrorist financing purposes. [4]

The Plan has two main objectives:

1. PREVENT THE MOVEMENT OF FUNDS AND IDENTIFY TERRORIST FUNDING:

   Key actions:
   - Ensure virtual currency exchange platforms are covered by the AntiMoney Laundering Directive;
   - Tackle terrorist financing through anonymous pre-paid instruments such as pre-paid cards;
   - Improve access to information and cooperation between EU Financial Intelligence Units;
   - Ensure a high level of safeguards for financial flows from high risk third countries;
   - Give EU Financial Intelligence Units access to centralised bank and payment account registers and central data retrieval systems.

2. DISRUPT SOURCES OF REVENUE FOR TERRORIST ORGANISATIONS:

   Key actions:
   - Tackle terrorist financing sources such as the illicit trade in goods, cultural goods and wildlife.
   - Work with third countries to ensure a global response to tackling terrorist financing sources

---

[4] See: http://ec.europa.eu/justice/criminal/files/aml-factsheet_en.pdf

The EU and national governments decided to bring extra precautions against terrorism financing activities after the events in Paris, France (European Commission Factsheet, Feb 2016). These precautions combined formed EU Action Plan.

The EU's Action Plan has 2 purposes:

1. To identify and prevent the transfer of Terrorist Funding by
   - Guaranteeing that the AML directive is applied on cyber currency exchange platforms
   - Investigating on anonymous pre-paid instruments
   - Expanding the information access between EU Financial Intelligence Units
   - Applying more precautions for high risk third countries' financial transfers
   - Expanding the authority of EU Financial Intelligence Units to access central bank's data and payment account registers.
2. To dislocate Income Sources for Terrorist Financing Groups by
   - Confronting the sources of the illegal activity (trade in wildlife, cultural goods)
   - Collaborating with third countries to have a worldwide response to reveal the sources of terrorist funding.

In Feb 2016, European Commission published a factsheet about an action plan to fight terrorism funding. The action plan indicates things to do in 2016 and 2017 to combat financing terrorism. [5]

EU Action Plan

The action plan is designed to gather EU countries working together to prevent funding criminal activities.

"The recent terrorist attacks on Europe's people and values were coordinated across borders, showing that we must work together to resist these threats" (European Commission President Jean-Claude Juncker).

According to the action plan for 2016 and 2017, some steps are needed to be taken immediately as a criminal action preventative strategy.

---

[5] See: http://europa.eu/rapid/press-release_IP-16-202_en.htm

1. Immediate Actions
   - Accelerate the UN's application with improved exchange of information and fast implementation on freezing procedures by the EU.
   - Provide technical support to third countries for them to keep up with UN procedures such as asset freezing, authorizations and permissions.

In addition to the immediate actions, EU commission also divides 2016 into two parts. In the first half of 2016, the commission aims to apply and update existing laws to prevent terrorist financing and transferring the illegal funds.

First Half of 2016's Actions

- Create a list to spot high-risk third countries that have shortages to fight terrorist financing and money laundering.
- Create a plan to stop wildlife trafficking.
- Include the issues below within the EU Anti-money Laundering Directive:
  - Design improved measures for high-risk third countries.
  - Avoid the risks of cyber currency exchange boards and pre-paid transactions.
  - Offer electronic data recovery systems or payment account records and a central bank.
  - Improve Financial Intelligence Unit's access to information
  - Improve the exchange of information between units (the Commission, the member states, and economic hands) on how to apply the preventive measures.

The Second half of 2016's Actions

The second half of 2016 action plan is designed by EU commission to imply new initiatives to strengthen the existing legal outline. In addition to that, the commission wanted to help third world countries to prevent and fight terrorist financing.

- Help high-risk regions like North Africa, South East Asia and Middle East to display and prevent terrorist financing activities.
- Provide technical support to high-risk regions to fight cultural goods trafficking using terrorist linkages.
- Accelerate the application date for the Fourth AML Directive.
- Offer new EU legislation to tone the illegal money-laundering agreements.
- Offer new EU legislation to prevent illegal fund transfers and assets transportation across borders.
- Evaluate the necessity for a new EU legislation on freezing the assets of terrorists within the borders of EU.
- Contribute all EU Member States on recognition of freezing and confiscating terrorists' assets.
- Introduce new measures to EU-US Terrorist Finance Tracking Programme.

In 2017, the goal is to identify terrorist financing activities and target the sources of criminal activities.

1. 2017 Actions

- Writing a money laundering and terrorism financing report including recommendations.
- Publishing the report to Member States to guide and warn them on illegal activities.
- Strengthening the power of authorities to fight the illegal trade of terrorists by offering a new legislation.

Cash Movement Controls

The Regulation accepted in 2005 and applied in 2007 controls the cash movements into and out of the European Union. According to that Regulation:

- Travelers need to make a declaration to customs authorities when entering or leaving the EU and carrying EUR 10,000 (or its equivalent in other currencies or easily convertible assets as checks drawn on third party) or more (Tavares, 2010).

Member countries must keep the records of the information collected from the declaration. Members also need to make those records available to the authorities to combat terrorist financing and money laundering.

United Nations (UN) Conventions Regarding Financial Institutions

The Vienna Convention:

The Vienna convention signed in 1988 under the protection of United Nations and became effective in 1990, is against Illicit Traffic in Narcotic Drugs and Psychotropic Substances. This agreement was signed by European Union and G-7 countries. Countries signed the agreement agreed to join to combat drug trafficking and laundering the earnings of the activity.

The success of the Convention depended on the mutual assistance and synchronization between the countries as there was variety in languages, and legal environments within the union. UN has developed two models for countries to implement the arrangements against money laundering. These models were:

a. The United Nations Model Agreement on Mutual Assistance in Criminal Matters, and
b. The United Nations Model Agreement on Extradition.

Both of the models were designed to distinguish the differences within the legal systems and the relations between them.

The Palermo Convention[6]:

The Convention was against Transnational Organized Crime, signed in 2001.

Merida Convention:

The Convention was against Corruption, signed in 2005

UN had defined the topics for fighting against money laundering. As a result of this directive the member states were expected to ensure that:

- money laundering is forbidden,
- customer identifications should be confirmed and records should be kept,
- suspicious transactions should be monitored and checked,
- institutions should co-operate with the authorities by reporting suspicious transactions and relevant information,
- suspects should not know that they are under investigation,
- anyone reporting a suspicious transaction should be protected from the breach of confidence actions,
- Institutions should implement and maintain sufficient systems of internal controls and employee training.

Basel Committee on Banking Regulations

The Basel Committee on Banking Supervision (BCBS) is a committee of banking supervisory authorities that was established by the central bank governors of the Group of 10 countries in 1975 (Bank of International Settlements).

---

[6] See: https://www.unodc.org/documents/middleeastandnorthafrica/organised-crime/
UNITED_NATIONS_CONVENTION_AGAINST_TRANSNATIONAL_OR-
GANIZED_CRIME_AND_THE_PROTOCOLS_THERETO.pdf

The Committee's member countries are,

- Argentina, Australia,
- Belgium, Brazil,
- Canada, China,
- European Union
- Hong Kong SAR
- France,
- Germany,
- Hong Kong SAR,
- India, Indonesia, Italy,
- Japan,
- Korea,
- Luxembourg,
- Mexico,
- Netherlands,
- Russia,
- Saudi Arabia, Singapore, South Africa, Spain, Sweden, Switzerland,
- Turkey,
- The United Kingdom and
- The United States.

In December 1988, the Basel Committee on Banking Supervision issued a "statement of principles" which international banks of member states are expected to fulfill. These principles were the basic rules for banking system which will make the authorities to track money laundering activities. The principles were covering the subjects as:

- identifying customers,
- avoiding processing of suspicious transactions, and
- Cooperating with law enforcement agencies.

While issuing these principles, the Committee stated the threat to public confidence in banks, and their stability that can occur if they unintentionally become associated with money laundering.

This document is related to the initial composition of the 1990 Forty Recommendations with its four major principles:

1. Know Your Customer (KYC),
2. Conduct business in compliance with high ethical standards and laws,
3. Cooperate fully with law enforcement authorities, and
4. Have in place policies and procedures to carry out the three principles above (Koh, 2006).

The International Monetary Fund (IMF)[7]

Money laundering and terrorism financing have effect on economy. Money laundering crime is considered as a profit-making crime involves the activities of:

- Drug and arm-trafficking,
- Corruption,
- Tax elusion, and
- Fraud.

These criminal activities generate a financial flow that affects the economy in a negative way. IMF has been active to prevent the negative effects of money laundering and terrorist financing on financial institutions and systems. According to Min Zhu Deputy Managing Director, IMF, 'Effective anti-money laundering and combating the financing of terrorism regimes are essential to protect the integrity of markets and of the global financial framework as they help mitigate the factors that facilitate the financial abuse'...

The activities achieved by IMF about Money laundering:

- In 2000, the work in the area of AML is expanded by international community.
- After September 11, 2001 AML activities are more expanded and included combating terrorism financing.

---

[7] See: http://www.imf.org/external/index.htm

- In 2009, the IMF initiated a trust fund to finance and support the activities in AML/CTF. Canada, France, Japan, Korea, Kuwait, Luxembourg, the Netherlands, Norway, Qatar, Saudi Arabia, Switzerland, and the United Kingdom committed to provide US$25. 3 million over 5 years to the financing of the Topical Trust Funds (TTF). The countries are expected to support the TTF to strengthen the global AML/CTF systems.
- In 2011, IMF reviewed the effectiveness of the Fund's in AML/CTF program and presented assistance for the future work.

The World Bank[8]

The purpose of the World Bank is to support client countries to strengthen their reliability in financial sectors with Technical Assistance, Policy Developments, and Assessments. To increase the awareness for preventing money laundering, the World Bank conducts regular trainings like the organizations as FATF and IMF. 'Lately, the World Bank delivers training for assessed countries for preparation to the assessments both on substance and processes.' The assessments are meant to identify the flaws in AML activities on country bases. The purpose of the assessments is to improve the country's framework in fighting against money laundering. Analyzed areas in assessments include:

- Legal and institutional,
- Supervisory and regulatory for the financial sector and other financial services providers, and
- International assistance.

The assessments need to follow certain regulations. 'All the assessments are conducted with reference to the FATF'S 40+9 Recommendations.'

---

[8] See: http://www.worldbank.org/

Turkey

Turkey is a significant money laundering country because of its geographical location.

Reasons for criminals' use of Turkey to launder money include:

1. Geographical Location (Middle-Eastern Region)

    -   Continuous conflict and war between Israel and Palestine,
    -   The ex-war between Iraq and Iran that took more than 7 years,
    -   The ongoing dispute and warfare between Turkey and illegal Kurdish terrorist organization PKK.

2. Turkey is on the main road for drug trafficking. Drug smugglers need a massive economy to serve, collect, and hide the funds within the financial market. Turkey plays an important role within the global economy with the potential and the infrastructure of the country, the available financial tools in its domestic market, and its role as a player in international markets.

3. The region is preferred for illegal arm trading especially for Islamic Terrorist organizations that trade guns. Several countries use Turkey for arms trafficking.

4. Turkey is in the middle of the OPEC (Organization of Petroleum Exporting Countries) and within this region unofficial oil trading is very common. However, the member countries are not fighting against the illegal oil trading because of economic and social reasons.

5. Turkey has a traditional habit of doing cash transactions. The habit creates an attractive environment for criminals to launder money via cash transactions. (See Tables 6.3 and 6.4)

According to MASAK's statistics August 2011, the sources and volumes of denunciation in Turkey between 2002 and 2006 are:

According to the data shown below between 2002 and 2006, banks (financial institutions) are developed in detecting and reporting money laundering cases. Financial sector has some different branches within. The improvement of the banks in tracking and reporting suspicious transactions is greater than the other financial institutions.

Table 6.3 Sources and volumes of money-laundering denunciations in Turkey

Source of Denunciation	2002	2003	2004	2005	2006	Total
Public Prosecutor Offices	168	171	218	178	93	828
Public Institutions	105	103	127	157	117	609
Banks	4	7	30	18	38	97
Press	1	1	4	8	4	18
Private Legal Staff	112	94	98	135	304	743
Abroad	3	4	6	4	7	24
Total	2395	2383	2487	2505	2569	2319

Source: MASAK Statistics, August 2011

Table 6.4 Suspicious Transactions Statistics of Financial Sector (Jan 2002-Dec 2006)

Source	2002	2003	2004	2005	2006	Total
Banks	193	177	288	349	1103	2110
Islamic Banks	0	3	1	2	30	36
Insurance Companies	1	0	0	0	0	1
Brokers	0	0	1	1	7	9
Total	194	180	290	352	1140	2156

Source: MASAK Statistics, August 2011

As we can see from the table, banks reporting suspicious transactions increased by 223% from 2005 to 2006 and.

Turkish government has introduced many measures to fight money-laundering activities targeting both financial and non-financial institutions. The measures cover:

- Incoming and outgoing fund transfers,
- Cross-border Currency Smuggling, and
- Purchasing high value objects such as gold, real estate or luxury cars.

Criminals can also launder money by:
- Weapon smuggling,
- Organ or Tissue smuggling,
- Smuggling of Historical Remaining,
- Fake Invoicing or related crimes,
- Crimes targeting to State's Identity, and
- Distributing fake money.

To prevent money laundering, knowing customers' identification becomes significant for financial institutions. Banks should require providing some acceptable documents for real and corporate clients' identification, like:

- For Persons
  - Turkish Citizens
    - Official ID
    - Driver's License
    - Passport
  - Foreigners
    - Passport
    - Residential Permit
- For Corporations
  - Registered in Turkey
    - Copy of commercial Entity Registration
    - Authorized Signature List of the authorities of the organization
  - Non-profit Organizations
    - Registration Certificates to the related government bodies.
  - Foundations or Other Entities
    - Documentation evidencing the activity of the organization.

CHAPTER 7

Two Money-Laundering Cases

Money Laundering in Turkey

Some cases that MASAK has shared with public to increase public's and authorities' awareness to such crimes include:

1. Historical Artifacts Smuggling

Transfers of large sums within the bank caused the research. MASAK found a criminal organization including 12 people who smuggled $300,000 of valued historical artifact. The sale proceeds were transferred to the criminals' bank accounts in Turkey. The bank in the country that launderers smuggled the historical artifacts from informed the bank in Turkey about the transfers. During the research related bank accounts were investigated by the authorities. The criminal were caught smuggling historical artifacts and could not present a rational declaration and document about the source of the transfers.

As a result, the authorities decided that $300,000 came from the criminal activity and transferred to the bank accounts to Turkey. The crime was reported to the Public Prosecutor's Office. The authorities sentenced the criminals and confiscated the financial proceeds.

2. Illegal Drug Trafficking

The case is reported by the Security Authorities to MASAK.

A citizen (X) of a foreign country, was involved in drug trafficking. He transferred the money that he obtained from the illegal activity to different bank accounts in many countries including Turkey. MASAK's investigation revealed that X transferred from $10,000 to $150,000 to

8 different people and 5 companies in Turkey. No documentation was justifying those transfers. As a result of the investigation, the companies and the accounts' owners were deemed to have sourced their funds from drug trafficking. The case was reported to the Public Prosecutor.

3. Receiving Undeserved Tax Refunds from the government

Some people received high sums of money in undeserved tax refunds from the government in the beginning of a fiscal year.

The United States Tax Administration investigated an incident of this kind during a tax audit and reported it to MASAK to investigate the event as a money laundering case. As a result of the investigation, MASAK found that three people, the Invoice maker, the Launderer, and the Restorer, invented an export organization to receive unjust tax refunds from the government.

- The Invoice maker provided fake invoices for the export firms in a different city resulting in the undeserved tax refunds. He also received a commission for the fake invoices he supplied to the firms and transferred the commissions to his relatives' bank accounts.
- The Launderer's role was to open bank accounts on behalf of his relatives' and his employees' name to disguise the source of the money that was obtained by a criminal activity.
- The last member of the criminal organization was the Restorer who acted as an accountant for the companies within the organization. He purchased a property with the money he gained on behalf of his wife.

As a result of the investigation, the members of the criminal organization were deemed to have received unjust tax refunds and gain illegal income. The criminals launder the earnings through purchasing various movable and immovable properties.

4. Gaining proceeds through coercion and intimidation.

A group of people took 10,000 TL [1]($3,388 USD), and a car from 6 people using coercion and intimidation. The case was sent for investigation to MASAK as a money laundering case.

---

[1]Turkish Lira [1 USD = 2.95 Turkish Lira] – August 2016

They were found to share those illegal proceeds. They also bought a new vehicle for their group with the remaining funds. The crime was detected and referred to the Public Prosecutor's Office.

Money Laundering in the Lebanese Canadian Bank

Federal Register 2011, the daily journal of the United States Government, provides information on a money laundering case in a Lebanese Canadian Bank.[2]

- Information about the bank:

The bank was located in Beirut, Lebanon and had the network of 35 branches in the same country. The representative office is located in Montreal, Canada. The bank has more than 600 employees and has the eighth largest assets among the other Lebanese banks. The privately owned bank was originally established in 1960 with the name as Banque des Activités Économiques. The financial institution provides a large range of financial and investment services to corporate and retail customers. The value of bank's total assets in 2009 was more than$5 billion.

In 2013 the Lebanese Canadian Bank agreed to pay $102 million in settlement after an investigation and legal action by the Drug Enforcement Administration and US Treasury and other US government authorities, which found that the Bank was involved in funding Hizbollah and other terrorist organizations and also money laundering for the narcotics community. The US authorities also believed that some of LCB's senior managers had assisted certain customers a scheme to launder narcotics payments by layering it cashflows related to used car trading between the United States and Africa, from which a share of cashflow was diverted to Hizbollah, but the US Authorities declined to reveal the basis for this claim and it was denied by Hizbollah. On 3 March 2011 it was announced that the bank was to merge with French bank Société

---

[2]Now defunct See: https://en.wikipedia.org/wiki/Lebanese_Canadian_Bank

Générale. The sale was effected by a transfer of most its assets to Société Générale's Lebanese unit.

- Information about Lebanon:

Lebanon has one of the most important banking sectors within the Middle Eastern region. According to the government treasury's information, the Lebanese banking system improved its asset quality, sustained sufficient liquidity and capitalization through the years. The major banks within the region also have relationships with U.S. financial institutions. Conversely, currency risks appear on the balance sheets of the banks. Moreover, the unstable political environment of the region creates an inefficient arena for banks to function. The country faces money laundering and terrorist financing activities because of its location and political instability according to U.S. department of States' Narcotics Control Strategy Report published in 2010. According to the World Bank, 21% of the Lebanese Gross Domestic Product (GDP) in 2009 of approximately $7billion USD is related with trade-based money laundering activities.

In addition to the information above,

- Lebanon has some important cash smuggling issues because of no cross-border currency reporting requirements.
- Lebanon has not agreed to the UN Convention which includes Suppression of the Financing of Terrorism. However, domestic laws forbid any activity that involves terrorism financing.
- Hezbollah, considered as a terrorist organization, which Lebanon calls a political party, is not subject to anti-terrorist financing laws. Consequently, in 1997 the United States government declared Hezbollah a Foreign Terrorist Organization. Moreover, in 2001, the terrorist organization was also designated as Specially Designated Global Terrorist by USA government.

Based on the information about the country and the bank, federal agencies and relevant divisions involved in the investigation of money laundering activities, suspected that the Lebanese Canadian Bank (LCB) was involved in money laundering activities. According to the US Financial Crimes Enforcement Network (FINCEN) report in 2011, money launderers functioning in countries in Europe, South America, Africa, and Middle East have utilized the bank. Apparently, the terrorist organization Hezbollah used the network for financial support to its illegal activities. In addition, the managers of the Lebanese Canadian Bank were aware of this situation and activities.

After revealing such criminal activities, FINCEN discovered that:

1. Drugs (Cocaine) are transported from Colombia and Panama to Europe and the Middle East through networks in Africa.
2. The funds raised from the drug sales went to Lebanon.
3. Money is moved to U. S. currency-based accounts to buy second-hand vehicles from American dealers.
4. The used vehicles were sent to Benin and Congo, Africa.
5. Finally, money obtained from the sales of the used vehicles went back to Lebanon.

At the end, the dirty money was laundered after the last step was completed.

Criminal activity's success may occur because of:

- Management support,
- Failure in internal controls, and
- The lack of banking rules application.

The Lebanon Canadian Bank lost its credibility because of its involvement in money laundering. The ownership of this financial institution has changed after the incident.

CHAPTER 8

Corporate Money-Laundering Events in USA

Many money-laundering cases are occurring around the world. However, revealing illegal actions requires investigation and knowing the customer. The cases below are examples that expose the money laundering activities and the actions taken by some banks. These examples are important for the reader to understand the span of money laundering activities.

Banamex USA

Banamex is a bank located in California, USA, operated as a U.S. division of Banco Nacional de Mexico. The bank, offered U.S. dollar credits to Mexican customers, and transferred money (credits) to Mexico or anywhere the customer wanted based on the agreement with Western Union. It became the third largest bank in the country when Citigroup acquired the Mexican bank in 2001 and operated it as a Commerce Bank, California for 5 years after the acquisition. However, Citigroup called the unit Banamex in 2006 to associate it with the Mexican market.

Antonio Peña Arguelles (Citigroup's Banamex, USA)

The article written by Alan Katz and Dakin Campbell, Bloomberg Markets in 2015 'Inside the Money Laundering scheme that Citibank Overlooked for Years' explain the money laundering case of Citigroup's Banamex, USA.

Antonio Peña Arguelles had a small business and wanted to open an account in Citigroup's Banamex USA in 2005. His business was breeding cattle and white-tailed deer, farm-raised for their grand antlers. According to the know-your-customer documents the bank requires, he expected $50 deposits to his account every month.

A week later, he transferred $7.09 million to his account in Citigroup's Banamex USA from an account in Mexico. The wired money happened to be drug money from Los Zetas, a cartel, formed by former Mexican soldiers. According to the banking regulators' report in 2013, Peña Arguelles smuggled $59.4 million through his account over a period of 8 years.

Banamex USA failed to notice this. The regulators' report also mentions Banamex USA's lack of investigation as of lacking suspicion even after the murder of Antonio Peña Arguelles's brother, Alfonso in 2011. Alfonso's body was discarded at the Christopher Columbus memorial in Nuevo Loredo, Mexico. The deceased body had a sign above him accusing money laundering and stealing from the cartel.

In August 2012, the Federal Deposit Insurance Corporation (FDIC) and the California Department of Business Oversight delivered a written order to bank Banamex USA to check some of its old bank accounts. However, Banamex USA has not taken any action about the subject matter until May 2013. Consequently, in May 2013, the FDIC and California Department of Business submitted to a confidential report about Banamex USA criticizing the company for not investigating the issue and solving the matter when possible with $32 million of a budget to correct the problems for that year.

The Peña Arguelles case states that Banamex USA has avoided inspecting the money transfers between US and Mexico branches. As a result of the detection of money-laundering activity, the bank had to pay $925 million to US government and $700 million to customers (*Inside the Money Laundering Scheme that Citi Overlooked for Years*, Bloomberg markets, Nov 2015).

What happened at Citigroup after money laundering transaction is revealed?

- In 2015, employees increased by 15%, to 30,000 in regulatory and compliance functions.
- In May 2015, the company agreed to pay $925 million to the U.S government.
- In July 2015, Citigroup agreed on paying $700 million to customers for illegal activities associated with the supplementary credit card products.

Citigroup is investigated by Justice Department about money-laundering activities at Banamex USA. The Federal Reserve and the Office of the Comptroller of the Currency departments also checked Citigroup's anti-money-laundering activities.

Sonia de Pau

In 2012, Sonia De Pau, a Mexican housewife, opened an account at the Texas branch of Banamex U.S. According to a 2013 FDIC report, she wanted to save money in USDs and spend it for her personal needs.

In November 2012 Sonia de Pau deposited a $25,000 check and she deposited 4 other checks worth $1.44 million 11 days after depositing the first one.

The International Bank of Commerce issued the checks.

What happened after?

Bank employees discovered the deposits before Sonia de Pau transferred the money out of her account. On Dec 3 2012, Banamex USA contacted its Mexican branch and warned it about the customer's account activity. De Pau's account was blocked by a legal order. However, Banamex USA did not take any further action until Dec 20, and found that most of the money was wired out of de Pau's account. A 2013 FDIC Report stated that, on Dec 20, Banamex USA filed a suspicious activity report with the U.S. Treasury's Financial Crimes Enforcement Network and the report had missing information about the withdrawn money on De Pau's account. A FDIC report in 2013 also stated that, after the initial report, Banamex USA ignored to review the ongoing suspicious activity and prevented law enforcement from tracking the deposited funds.

FDIC sent a consent order to Banamex USA before issuing the formal agreement in August 2012. The order was sent to inform the bank about what needed to be fixed. However, according to the FDIC 2013 report, Banamex management failed to show interest in detecting or reporting suspicious money transfers until mid-2013.

In 2015, Citigroup's Mexico unit received a subpoena by the Justice Department in addition to an investigation on Banamex USA about the fund transfers between the US and Mexico units of the bank.

As the investigation follows, employees were questioned and revealed the overlooked actions. The CEO of the bank has changed in 2013 right after the federal's consent order. The new CEO, Rebecca Macieira-Kaufmann, brought new rules to the bank to avoid future money-laundering activities.

Banamex USA had $3 million in assets whereas Citigroup's assets were $1.8 trillion.[1] Banamex, as the largest global subsidiary of Citigroup, damaged Citigroup's reputation with its $400 million fraud loans. Furthermore, Citigroup had more money laundering issues long before these cases.

According to the U.S. General Accounting Office report 1998, in the mid-1990's, the bank transferred more than $100 million from the accounts of Raúl Salinas, the brother of Mexico's former president, to accounts in Switzerland and United Kingdom. In addition to that, Banamex also concealed the source of this money. In 2001, after U.S. law enforcement officials revealed this money-laundering activity, the bank had to pay $7.7 million in penalties to the U.S. government.

---

[1] See present (2016) balance sheet at: http://www.ibanknet.com/scripts/callreports/getbank.aspx?ibnid=usa_750864

CHAPTER 9

New Place to Launder Money

CHINA

According to Erika Kinetz, based on recent police investigations and lawsuits in Europe and U.S., China is offering many money-laundering methods (Kinetz, 2016). Some are,

- Import and export activities,

Using bank accounts in China and Hong Kong, three Columbians located in China, laundered over a $5 billion US for drug cartels in Mexico and Columbia. The money was used to purchase fake goods (copies of expensive brands in clothes, shoes, bags, etc.) in China which were later shipped to Columbia and other export markets.

- Informal money transfers,

Fei Gian (flying money) is an illegal money transfer method Israeli networks use to launder money through Chinese immigrants across Europe. Chinese immigrants give their money to a member of the local Chinese community in European countries like France, Spain, Italy, Germany, or Belgium. The Chinese community member, also called as the bagman, provides bank account information in China to the Israeli contact. After ensuring that money was transferred to the right account, the bagman pays the Israeli fraudsters.

- Cyber- scamming.

Cyber scamming is impersonating top corporate executives by creating a fake president, CEO, or corporate e-mails to trick Western companies. FBI reports that, within 2 years, scammers had conned $1.8 million US by using this method. The criminals are not necessarily Chinese however, the funds collected illegally, are transferred to the banks in China and Hong Kong.

CHAPTER 10

Measures for Preventing Money Laundering

To separate clients form money launderers and criminals some measures need to be implemented by financial institutions.

- Know Your Customer (KYC)
- Keep Records
- List down possible suspicious transactions

Customer Identification principle is the most important step for differentiating customers from launderers in banks. The purpose of this procedure is to ensure openness and transparency in customer transactions. FATF has some regulations for financial institutions to apply to prevent organizations from money-laundering activities. Banks should follow the rules about their clients below for their safety:

- Knowing the customers' real identity and address,
- Checking the validity of the customers' documents and information,
- Knowing the reasons of the customers' preference of the bank and the purpose of opening an account within the financial institution,
- Knowing the profession, main profit-based activities, and professional principles of the client,
- Knowing the capacity of the customers' transactions,
- Knowing the suppliers or the buyers of the client,
- Knowing the location of the customers' office.

Besides the principles above financial institutions also need to follow some principles to maintain their protection from money laundering:

- Financial Institutions should receive customer information forms from each client including persons and organizations. Customers' information on the forms could be shared under the needed circumstances. The clients should fill up the information forms based on trust and transparency.
- Financial institutions should not open any kind of bank account with missing information or an anonymous name.
- Banks should screen and keep the records of the accounts to check if they are used by the client with a name associated to the account.
- Banks should not accept to open an account under the name of a third person or more than one person. If the client can legally authorize to issue such transaction and the reasons for that transaction are reasonable, then the bank can approve the process.
- General instructions should be certified by the notary. The documents subject to a transaction should be confirmed by the related organization.
- In minors' accounts age restrictions should be applied.

Developing Challenges in Turkish Money Laundering Applications

According to the gathered data of MASAK December 2011, The Turkish money-laundering regulations haven't been merged with Directive 2005/60/EC yet. The 2005 directive is about 'the prevention of the use of the financial system for the purpose of money laundering and terrorist financing' . . . On the other hand, the Law of Prevention of Laundering of the Proceeds of Crime includes regulations for avoiding the purpose of using the financial systems for money-laundering activities is supported by the Directive 91/308/EEC.

Certain types of transactions require improved measures, notably:

- Large and complex transactions, and
- Transactions with no rational financial purpose.

While undertaking such transactions, the involved sides should keep the records and documents to present the information to the related authorities when needed.

Technology could be very useful for criminals to launder money. For that reason, involved parts within a financial transaction should take some precautions against technological risks. Financial institutions need to pay special attention when depositing cash in bank accounts, withdrawing cash, and transferring money electronically. Financial institutions also need to pay attention while establishing trade relations with people or organizations. Involved parties should collect information about the transaction and the other side to protect their side from money-laundering type of activities.

In addition to the informationabove, FATF has pointed some additional requirements about Turkey's money-laundering regulations. According to FATF, MASAK should start providing feedback according to STR's requirements. The feedback report should include when and how to report suspicious transactions. According to FATF's published public statement in 2011, Turkey is in the list of the countries that have not progressed in addressing the deficiencies or an action plan to point out those flaws. These deficiencies include the crime of financing terrorist activities and implementation of legal outline for identifying and preventing terrorist activities.

Conclusion and Recommendations

Improving MLA regulations may contribute to increasing the awareness about the way financial institutions manage their AMLs activities and the potential negative financial consequences of MLAs to the economy of a country. They might also provide information about different money laundering methods and how to mitigate them.

Money laundering activities do not only emanate from terrorist or criminal groups. Indeed, money laundering may also emanate from financial activities such as: avoiding tax payments.

Applying anti-money laundering activities is necessary for financial organizations to meet the legal requirements. AML regulations could prevent unwanted results as follows:

- Reduction of investor confidence because of the country's reduced financial market credibility.
  Countries with high money laundering ratios also have low investment ratios because of the lack of trust that investors have for those countries' financial markets.
- Affecting one country's financial market.
  This situation increases the risk of the involved financial institutions' position in the market and may result in its bankruptcy.
- Economic crisis in the country where MLA takes place.
  Financial crises may also affect other countries that have business relations with the source country.
- Change in assets and liabilities that may affect the financial situation of the affected financial organization.
- Instability in money demand within in affected countries.

- Large variation of various currencies.

Launderers would use different type of money transactions to launder their funds. Criminals would transfer money in and out of the country and exchange the currency several times to achieve their goals. The situation would result in financial instability when large variation of money is entering a country.

- Unbalanced income distribution.

Laundering money involves other financial crimes such as tax evasion because the source of the money is not official and legal.

Money laundering activities would also decrease people's welfare within a country. Citizens would not be comfortable and happy in the country they are living in. The gap between high and low- income people would be high. People would question the financial, political, and social system as they discover the inequalities that those systems create. The dissimilarity in life standards would affect people's life emotionally as well. People would become unsatisfactory and unhappy as a result of the high ratio of money laundering activities in their countries.

To prevent the effect of illegal financial and political activities, people should support the regulations and policies governments' aim to apply. Negative results of illegal activities would motivate people to develop and implement additional solutions to prevent the effects of money laundering actions.

People can research the organizations in detail before sending or receiving funds.

Money laundering is an international problem. In a global finance system, countries with ML problems affect each other. Governments and financial institutions cannot prevent money laundering only by themselves. People should be aware of the problem and support the AML regulations with no hesitation.

References

Action Plan To Strengthen the fight Against Terrorist Financing. (2016). European Commission. Retrieved from http://ec.europa.eu/justice/criminal/files/aml-factsheet_en.pdf

Aiolfi, G; Dobovcek, B; Klemencic, G; Lebeaux, V; Ledergerber, Z; Loo, W;Moehrenshlager, M; Pontifex, B; Savran, O; Uriarte, C; Zudova, O. (2008). *Corruption: A Glossary of International Standards of Criminal Law.* OECD Publications.

Alexander, R. (2007). Insider Dealing and Money Laundering In the EU: Law and Regulation. University of London, UK.

Annand, A. (2011). Combating Terrorist Financing: Is Canada's Legal Regime Effective? University of Toronto Law Journal.

Baker, R. (2010). *Transparency First.* The American Interest. (p 58–65).

Bank for International Settlements.

Bank Regulatory Compliance Officer Job Description. Retrieved from www.advisoryhq.com

Borekci, H.; Erol, C. (2011). Assessment of Turkey's Anti-Money Laundering and Combating Terrorism Financing System, Vol 6, Issue 23, pg 3748–3768. Journal of Yasar University.

China now Global Hub for Money Laundering. Times Colonist. (2016, Mar 29) Pg. B3. Retrieved from http://digital.timescolonist.com/epaper/viewer.aspx?noredirect=true

Delston, R. S., and Walls, S. C. (2009). Reaching Beyond Banks: How to Target Trade-Based Money Laundering and Terrorist Financing Outside the Financial Sector. The Case Western Reserve Journal of International Law.

Erdilek, A. (2007). Turkey's Unregistered Economy. In Today's Zaman. Retrieved from http://www.todayszaman.com/columnistDetail_getNewsById.action?newsId=103210

Federal Deposit Insurance Corporation. FDIC and CDBO Assess Civil Money Penalties Against Banamex, USA, Century City, CA. (2015, July 22). Retrieved from https://www.fdic.gov/news/news/press/2015/pr15061.html

Federal Deposit Insurance Corporation. (2015, July 22). Washington, DC. Retrieved from http://www.dbo.ca.gov/Press/press_releases/2015/Joint_Stipulation_and_Order_to_Pay_Civil_Money_Penalty_07-22-15.pdf

Federal Reserve System Reports. New York. Retrieved from http://www.federalreserve.gov/boarddocs/press/bhc/2001/20010716/attachment.pdf

Ferwerda, J. (2009). The Economics of Crime and Money Laundering: Does Anti-Money Laundering Policy Reduce Crime? Tjalling C. Koopmans Research Institute, Discussion Paper Series 08–35.

Financial Crimes Enforcement Network. (2011). Finding that the Lebanese Canadian Bank is a Financial Institution of Primary Money Laundering Concern. Retrieved from https://www.fincen.gov/statutes_regs/patriot/pdf/LCBNoticeofFinding.pdf

Giraldo, J; Trinkunas, H. (2007). *Terrorism Financing and State Responses.* Stanford University Press, California.

Gordon, Richard K. (2011). Losing the War against Dirty Money: Rethinking Global Standards on Preventing Money Laundering and Terrorism Financing. Faculty Publications. Paper 148. Retrieved from http://scholarlycommons.law.case.edu/faculty_publications/148

Internal Revenue Service (IRS), (2011). Bank Secrecy Act. Retrieved from https://www.irs.gov/businesses/small-businesses-self-employed/bank-secrecy-act

Inside the Money Laundering Scheme that Citi Overlooked for Years. (2015, Nov 20). Bloomberg markets. Retrieved from http://www.bloomberg.com/news/articles/2015-11-20/inside-the-money-laundering-scheme-that-citi-overlooked-for-years

Jojarth, C. (2009). Crime, War and GlobalTrafficking: *Designing International Cooperation.* New York, Cambridge University Press.

Koh, J. (2006). Suppressing Terrorist Financing and Money Laundering. Germany, Springer Berlin.

Kumar, D. (2009). *Money Laundering Activities Around The World.* Retrieved from http://www.saching.com/Article/Money-laundering-activities-around-the-world/3102

Layton, J. (2006). *How Money Laundering Works.* Retrieved from http://money.howstuffworks.com/money-laundering.htm

Le-Khac, N; Markos, S; Kechadi, M. (2009). A Heuristics Approach for Fast Detecting Suspicious Money Laundering Cases in an Investment Bank. World Academy of Science, Engineering and Technology International Journal of Computer, Electrical, Automation, Control and Information Engineering Vol: 3, No:12. Bangkok, Thailand.

Lormel, D. (2007). Understanding and Disrupting Terrorist Financing.

Lo, C. (2002). FATF Initiatives To Combat Terrorist Financing. OECD Observer No 231/232. Retrieved from http://www.oecdobserver.org/news/archivestory.php/aid/717/FATF_initiatives_to_combat_terrorist_financing.html

Low Kim Cheng, P. (2010). Anti-money laundering + Knowing your Customer =Plain Business Sense. Insights to a Changing World Journal, Issue 4, p131

MASAK Statistics. August 2011. Retrieved from the website http://www.masak .gov.tr/tr

MASAK. Suspicious Transactions Guideline. Retrieved from http://www.masak .gov.tr/en/content/suspicious-transactions-types/1329

McSkimming, S. (2009). Trade-Based Money Laundering: Responding To an Emerging Threat. (p 37–63). Deaken Law Review.

Morris-Cotterill, N. (1999). *Use and Abuse of the Internet in Fraud and* Money Laundering International Review of Law Computers and Technology. Vol 13, issue 2, pg 211–228.

Olsen, William P. (2010). The Anti-Corruption Handbook: How To Protect Your Business In The Global Marketplace. John Wiley & Sons, Inc., Hoboken, New Jersey.

Quirk, Peter J. (1997). Money Laundering: Muddying the Macroeconomy. Finance and Development. International Monetary Fund. Vol. 34, No.1 Retrieved from http://www.imf.org/external/pubs/ft/fandd/1997/03/pdf/quirk.pdf

Pickert, K. (2009). A Brief History of The Tamil Tigers. Retrieved from http://content.time.com/time/world/article/0,8599,1869501,00.html

Reider-Gordon, M. (2011). US and International Anti-Money Laundering Developments. *The International Lawyer*, Vol 45, No 1, pg 365–379. Retrieved from http://www.jstor.org/stable/23644019

Reuter, P. ; Truman, E. (2004). Chasing dirty money: The fight Against Money Laundering. Washington, DC: Institute for International Economics.

Rietbroek, S. (2009). Emerging money laundering methods: Digital precious metals. Retrieved from http://themonetaryfuture.blogspot.com.tr/2010/02/ digital-precious-metals-consistently.html

Roberge, I. (2007). Misguided Policies in the War on Terror? The Case for Disentangling Terrorist Financing From Money Laundering. College Glendon, University York.

Rudner, M. (2010). Hizbullah Terrorism Finance: Fund-Raising and Money-Laundering. Studies in Conflict and Terrorism, Volume 33 Issue 8, page 700–715.

Sharman, J. C. and Chaikin, D. (2009). Corruption and Anti-Money-Laundering Systems: Putting a Luxury Good to Work. Governance, Volume 22, Issue 1, page 27–45

Schuman Associates. Anti-Money Laundering Europe. Retrieved from http://www. amleurope.com/index.php/news-2/65-eu-action-plan-to-fight-against-terrorist-financing

Solin, M; Zerzan, A. (2010). Mobile Money: Methodology for Assessing Money Laundering and Terrorist Financing Risks. The GSM Association. Retrieved from http://tools.ietf.gsma.com/mobilefordevelopment/wp-content/uploads/2012/06/ amlfinal58.pdf

Tavares, C; Thomas, G. (2010). *Money Laundering In Europe. Report of Work Carried out By* Eurostat and DG Home Affairs. Retrieved from http://www.fi.ee/failid/Money_Laundering_in_Europe_Eurostat_and_DG_Home_Affairs_2010.pdf

The Economist (2001). Through the Wringer. Banks are doing more than ever before to clamp down on money laundering but is it enough? New York. Retrieved from http://www.economist.com/node/568832

The Fourth EU Anti Money Laundering Directive. (2015). Deloitte and Touche. Retrieved from https://www2.deloitte.com/content/dam/Deloitte/ie/Documents/FinancialServices/investmentmanagement/ie_2015_The_Fourth_EU_Anti_Money_Laundering_Directive_Deloitte_Ireland.pdf

The Washington Post. (2012). Canadian Who Admitted Trying to Help now-defeated Tamil Tigers Sentenced in NY to Time Served. Published by Associated Press, New York. Retrieved from http://www.cnsnews.com/news/article/time-served-canadian-ny-tamil-tiger-case

The United Nations Office on Drugs and Crime (UNODC). Retrieved from https://www.unodc.org/unodc/en/money-laundering/laundrycycle.html

Vaughn, B; Chanlett-Avery, E; Lum, T; Manyin, M; Niksch, L. (2008). *Terrorism in Southeast Asia*. Nova Science Publishers, New York.

Vlacek, W. (2007). Surveillance to Combat Terrorist Financing in Europe: Whose Liberty, Whose Security? European Security, Volume 16, issue 1, page 99–119.

World Compliance, (2008). Retrieved from http://www. worldcompliance. com/money-laundering. html, last accessed in 2016.

Yang and Wei (2010). Detecting money laundering using filtering techniques: a multiple-criteria index. Journal of Economic Policy Reform, vol 13, issue 2, pg 159–178.

Yavuz, E. (2009). Turkey's Efforts Fall Short in Combating Money Laundering. Today's Zaman.

Yen, Z. (2005). Anti-Money Laundering Requirements: Costs, Benefits, and Perceptions. London, England. Retrieved from http://www.zyen.com/PDF/AMLR_FULL.pdf

Zdanowicz, J. (2004). Detecting Money Laundering and Terrorist Financing via Data Mining. Communications of the ACM. Vol 47, No 5, pg 53–55.

Index

OTHER TITLES IN OUR FINANCE AND FINANCIAL MANAGEMENT COLLECTION

John A. Doukas, Old Dominion University, *Editor*

- *Get Rich Slow: Your Guide to Producing Income & Building Wealth with Rental Real Estate* by John Webber
- *Venture Capital in Asia: Investing in Emerging Countries* by William Scheela
- *Global Mergers and Acquisitions: Combining Companies Across Borders* by Abdol S. Soofi and Yuqin Zhang
- *The Fundamentals of Financial Statement Analysis as Applied to the Coca-Cola Company* by Carl B. McGowan, Jr., John C. Gardner, and Susan E. Moeller
- *Corporate Valuation Using the Free Cash Flow Method Applied to Coca-Cola* by Carl B. McGowan, Jr.
- *Capital Budgeting* by Sandeep Goel
- *Online Marketing to Investors: How to Develop Effective Investor Relations* by Daniel R. Valentine
- *Essentials of Retirement Planning: A Holistic Review of Personal Retirement Planning Issues and Employer-Sponsored Plans, Third Edition* by Eric J. Robbins
- *Redefining Shareholder Value: Demystifying the Valuation Myth* by Mariana Schmid and Milan Frankl
- *Financial Ratios* by Sandeep Goel
- *Financial Services Sales Handbook: A Professionals Guide to Becoming a Top Producer* by Clifton T. Warren

Announcing the Business Expert Press Digital Library

Concise e-books business students need for classroom and research

This book can also be purchased in an e-book collection by your library as

- *a one-time purchase,*
- *that is owned forever,*
- *allows for simultaneous readers,*
- *has no restrictions on printing, and*
- *can be downloaded as PDFs from within the library community.*

Our digital library collections are a great solution to beat the rising cost of textbooks. E-books can be loaded into their course management systems or onto student's e-book readers.

The **Business Expert Press** digital libraries are very affordable, with no obligation to buy in future years. For more information, please visit **www.businessexpertpress.com/librarians**. To set up a trial in the United States, please contact **sales@businessexpertpress.com**.

www.ingramcontent.com/pod-product-compliance
Lightning Source LLC
Chambersburg PA
CBHW071105210326
41519CB00020B/6167